SIR GAWAIN

AND THE

GREEN KNIGHT

Medieval European Studies XIII

Patrick W. Conner, Series Editor

Other Titles in the Series:

Sir Gawain
and the
Green Knight

A CLOSE VERSE TRANSLATION

TRANSLATED BY

Larry D. Benson

WITH A FOREWORD AND

MIDDLE ENGLISH TEXT EDITED BY

DANIEL DONOGHUE

MORGANTOWN 2012

West Virginia University Press, Morgantown 26506

Copyright 2012 by West Virginia University Press

All rights reserved

First edition published 2012 by West Virginia University Press

Printed in the United States of America

20 19 18 17 16 15 14 13 12   9 8 7 6 5 4 3 2 1

Paper: 978-1-933202-89-1 / EPUB: 978-1-935978-10-7

PDF: 978-1-935978-63-3

Library of Congress Cataloguing-in-Publication Data

Benson, Larry D. 19——

Sir Gawain and the Green Knight : a close verse translation / by Larry D. Benson. -- 1st ed.

p.   cm. -- (Medieval European studies ; v. 13)

Includes both the modern English and the Middle English text.

Includes bibliographical references.

ISBN-13: 978-1-933202-89-1 (pbk. : alk. paper)

ISBN-13: 978-1-935978-10-7 (electronic)

1. Gawain (Legendary character)--Romances. 2. Knights and knighthood--Poetry.

3. Arthurian romances. I. Benson, Larry Dean, 1929- II. Title.

PR2065.G3A332 2012

821'.1--dc23

Library of Congress Control Number: 2011018426

Book Design by Than Saffel

Background image: Willow Bough wallpaper designed by William Morris, repurposed as fabric design c. 1895. Used under a Creative Commons license granted by PKM, the original scanner. Source: http://en.wikipedia.org/wiki/File:Morris_Willow_Bough_1887.jpg . Front cover image: Wood-cut of a Knight. (From Caxton's *Game of the Chess*) Source: Knight, Charles: "Old England: A Pictorial Museum" (1845).

Contents

Acknowledgments

Both of us owe thanks to Pat Conner for initiating the process by which West Virginia University Press undertook this publication. Daniel thanks Larry for the invitation to collaborate and for good conversations over Mexican food. Larry owes thanks to many, such as Jim Smith, who helped often without knowing it. But his greatest help came from Stephen A. Barney, who generously took the time to read and correct the whole manuscript. So too did Theodore M. Andersson, whose careful reading saved Larry from many blunders. Finally, the translation is dedicated to Gavin Benson, whose very name bears witness to his long and happy association with the best of knights.

Foreword

By Daniel Donoghue

W hen Larry Benson first described his project to translate *Sir Gawain and the Green Knight*, I was skeptical. It wasn't just the thought that other translations have appeared in recent years. "Why another?" is easily answered if the translation is good, and Benson has every credential a translator needs, because his ties to the poem are deep and go back at least to his now-classic 1965 book, *Art and Tradition in Sir Gawain and the Green Knight*. No, my skepticism had to do with the kind of translation he proposed, which keeps as much of the original language as possible but in modernized spelling, and which substitutes modern equivalents for words in the poem's diction that have fallen out of use. Its adherence to the literal is what makes it a "Close Translation." To me it seemed like a high-risk formula: neither fish nor fowl, a gallimaufry of modern and medieval, a mechanical process applied to a living work of art. Was it a real translation or a kind of aggressive normalization? On a more practical level, does modern English have suitable equivalents for the *Gawain*-poet's famously rich word-hoard of synonyms?

Then I read it. My skepticism yielded to acceptance, acceptance to admiration, admiration to reading pleasure. This translation really *is* the closest thing to reading the Middle English poem because of its consistency in preserving the essential features of the original: its rhythm, its alliteration, and its unique syntax. Recent translations by Borroff, Tolkien, Merwin, and Armitage craft an alliterative verse line as an aesthetic echo and homage to the original; O'Donoghue's does away with alliteration but keeps the pattern of four prominent stresses per line. No matter what style of verse line is chosen, each successful translation like these stands on its own two feet and invites the reader to enter into a temporary conspiracy to forget about the original. This amnesia is both a product of the poet's craft and a sign of success. Benson's literal translation, however, replaces this illusion with a sense of proximity. It never lets readers forget that they are reading a translation, because the original never seems out of earshot. While the meaning of each line is comprehensible even to students coming to the poem for the first time, the translation retains the essence of the poem's alliterative lines (which in this edition are printed *en face*). Illustrative passages could be chosen almost at random, but the following description of Gawain and his guide making their predawn trip to the Green Chapel displays the main features:

> They bound by banks   where boughs are bare,
> They climb by cliffs   where clings the cold.
> The heaven was up high   but ugly there-under;
> Mist drizzled on the moor   melted on the mountains;
> Each hill had a hat,   a huge mantle of mist;
> Brooks boiled and broke   by banks about,
> Brightly shattering on shores   where they shot down.
> Well wild was the way   where they went by wood.
> (2077–84)

It is all here: the visual images, the narrative control, the compact phrasing, the rhythm and alliteration. A poetic rendering today could not venture phrasings such as "where clings the cold" and "Well wild was the way," but they rise naturally from the poem's wellspring. To see this translation's fidelity, compare the first two lines above with the original:

Þay boȝen bi bonkkeȝ þer boȝeȝ ar bare,
Þay clomben bi clyffeȝ þer clengeȝ þe colde.

Benson's translation also preserves what is called the historical present (illustrated here with "clings" as opposed to "clung") as well as older word forms like "thou keepest"; it keeps original features of syntax such as multiple negatives and the inversion of word order. Poetic synonyms such as *freke, gome, haþel, segge* which have fallen out of the language are replaced with a modern word alliterating on the same sound: *fighter, gallant, horseman, stalwart*. The effect of preserving syntax and diction can be sensed in a line like "The gallant upon Gringolet galloped them under" (748), where "gallant" is an unintrusive substitute and "them under" preserves the original's inversion of word order. Examining isolated instances does not do justice to the overall effect of reading passage after passage, where Benson's literal translation shows its great advantage in conveying the medieval poem's energy and excitement. It can be read for pure enjoyment, but it also appeals to those who want more direct engagement with the medieval text.

The Poem and the Poet

One of the masterpieces of Middle English, *Sir Gawain and the Green Knight* stands comparison with the greatest literature from any language and period. This critical reception, however, is fairly recent, because the poem did not come to the attention of a broad audience until the middle of the nineteenth century, when it was first edited and published. Unlike Chaucer, for example, whose poetic gifts were recognized in his lifetime and whose works survive in multiple copies, the *Gawain*-poet apparently never enjoyed wide circulation, and all that survives is contained in an unassuming manuscript, roughly the size of the book you are holding, now housed in the British Library with the shelf mark Cotton Nero A.x, Art 3. Besides the text translated here, the manuscript contains another three narrative poems almost certainly by the same author, which are known by their modern names *Pearl*, *Cleanness*, and *Patience*. The four poems' relatively obscure dialect, not surprisingly, has conditioned their modern reception. Most readers today encounter them only in translation, while Chaucer's London dialect, by contrast, is still relatively accessible to anyone familiar with Modern English.

Nothing is known of the *Gawain*-poet except what can be gleaned from his body of writings. They show he was a person of considerable learning. (I use "he" for convenience; among the things unknown is the poet's gender.) Parts of the plot of *Sir Gawain* reveal a deep acquaintance with French romances; his other poems show familiarity with Latin theology and biblical exegesis. The literary sources of all four poems, taken together, suggest that he had training appropriate for the clergy, but we cannot be sure whether he took orders or, if he did, whether he remained in religious life. The poet's imaginative world is vast and varied: *Sir Gawain* is a secular romance rather than a religious work; *Pearl* presents itself as a dream vision of a father who loses his daughter, yet this secular frame is used for a didactic message based on orthodox theology. *Patience and Cleanness*, by contrast, are more religious in a conventional sense. Even if the poet were ordained in higher orders, he knew enough about the outside world to write vivid scenes of boar hunting and sexual seduction. In thinking about this mixture of the sacred and profane from our historical remove, we need to remember that the secular and religious spheres in the Middle Ages existed in constant dynamic interaction. The clergy at this time could be quite worldly—worldly by our anachronistic standards.

Where did this cultivated poet live and write? The dialect of the four poems in Cotton Nero A.x point to Cheshire, not far from the where the northern borders of Wales touch England. In addition, some of the place names mentioned in *Sir Gawain* are found in northern Wales. Recent scholarship, however, has expanded the question of "where?" by pointing out that a number of the poem's themes would find special resonance in Richard II's royal court in London. Richard had long-standing ties to Cheshire and recruited hundreds of Cheshire men into his retinue (Mann 2009). While it is possible that the poem's primary audience were London transplants, their regional dialect is preserved in the language of *Sir Gawain* and the other three poems, which is quite unlike the London dialect. Linguistic and other evidence points to a date in the latter half of the fourteenth century, which makes the poet a contemporary of Chaucer, Gower, and Langland. There is no evidence his path ever crossed theirs, as tantalizing as the prospect might be in light of the possible London connection.

The Verse Form

If you will listen to this lay   but a little while
I shall tell it at once,   as I in town heard
            With tongue,
      As it is set down and struck
      In story stout and strong.
      With true letters interlocked
      In this land as has been long.   (30–36)

Sir Gawain and the Green Knight is but one of a number of substantial poems assigned to the fourteenth-century "Alliterative Revival." Most prevalent in the north and west of England, the Revival saw a flourishing of poems that use alliteration as an essential formal device. For centuries the alliterative line had been a traditional English verse form—as the quotation above puts it, "In this land as has been long"—as opposed to the rhyming iambic verse associated with French and other continental literatures. The alliterative line's persistence within an English oral tradition, though virtually certain, is untraceable for the obvious reason that it was spoken, not written. It descends from Old English alliterative verse in ways that are not entirely clear because the literary record is fragmentary. We do know, however, that already by the end of the Old English period the strict metrical conventions were changing. And later, after more than two centuries when poems like *SGGK* re-emerge "with true letters interlocked," the alliterative line has expanded and gained rhythmic flexibility. Because Benson's translation follows the original poem so closely, it can be used to illustrate *Sir Gawain*'s verse form.

The *Gawain*-poet's basic line unfolds into two parts, divided by a pause called a caesura. A typical half-line has two syllables that receive a prominent stress (or accent), and the number of unstressed syllables between them can vary, so that while the rhythm will always change from one line to the next, the pattern of four stressed syllables gives shape to each line. Usually the first three of the stressed syllables will alliterate but not the final one. The following lines, coming shortly after the passage of the ride to the Green Chapel quoted earlier, show the alliterating syllables in bold type:

With that the warrior in the wood   wrenches his bridle,
Hit the horse with his heels   as hard as he could,
Leaps him over the land   and leaves the knight there
(2152-54)

The poet occasionally takes liberties so that, for example, some lines have only two alliterating syllables and others have four, as shown in the three lines immediately preceding the passage just quoted:

"Now farewell, by God's wounds,   Gawain the noble!
For all the gold upon ground   I would not go with thee,
Nor bear thee fellowship through this forest   one foot further."
(2149–51)

Note how in the first line (2149) the first sounds of *God's* and *Gawain* carry primary alliteration, while the **w** of *farewell*, *wounds*, and the second half of *Gawain* add a second, subtle layer of alliteration. In the third line (2151), four words alliterate on *f*, including the final word *further*, which by traditional rules should not alliterate. These two examples only scratch the surface of the variability in the alliteration and rhythm of the lines throughout the poem. Some lines, for example, have more stressed syllables without alliteration, and a few have no alliteration at all (Borroff 1962).

The long alliterative line, however, is not the only kind of line in *Sir Gawain*. Each of its stanzas closes with a five-line coda, called a "bob and wheel," which begins with a two-syllable turn (the bob) leading to four trimeter lines (the wheel), which together follow the rhyme *a-b-a-b-a*. The following passage begins with the lines already given, which lead into the bob and wheel that ends the stanza:

"Now farewell, by **G**od's wounds   **G**awain the noble!
For all the **g**old upon **g**round   I would not **g**o with thee,
Nor bear thee **f**ellowship through this **f**orest   one *foot fur-*
ther."
With that the **W**arrior in the **W**ood   **W**renches his bridle,
Hit the **h**orse with his *h*eels   as **h**ard as he could,
Leaps him over the **l**and   and **l**eaves the knight there
                                    A**l**one.   *a*
                    "By God's self," quoth Gawain,   *b*
                    "I will neither gripe nor groan;   *a*
                    Of God's will I am certain,   *b*
                    And I know that I am His own."   *a*
                    (2149-59)

The alliterations and rhymes in the translation remain faithful wherever possible to the original Middle English, given here for the sake of comparison:

"Now fareȝ wel, on **G**odeȝ half,   **G**awayn þe noble!
For alle þe **g**olde vpon **g**rounde   I nolde **g**o wyth þe,
Ne bere þe **f**elaȝschip þurȝ þis **f**ryth   on **f**ote fyrre."
Bi þat þe **W**yȝe in þe **W**od   **W**endeȝ his brydel,
Hit þe **h**ors with þe **h**eleȝ   as **h**arde as he myȝt,
Lepeȝ hym ouer þe **l**aunde,   and **l**eueȝ þe knyȝt þere
                                    Alone.   *a*
                    "Bi Goddeȝ self," quoþ Gawayn,   *b*
                    "I wyl nauþer grete ne grone;   *a*

To Godde3 wylle I am ful bayn,   *b*

And to Hym I haf me tone."   *a*

(2149-59)

Many of the words from the original are simply repackaged with modern spellings (e.g., *nauþer* becomes *neither*), but the translation necessarily must make some adjustments. Note, for example, that in modern English the **w** of *wrenches* (2152) does not actually alliterate—call it eye-alliteration—because the initial sound in the pronunciation of the word is *r*; and the rhymes in the bob and tail are sometimes inexact, as with *Gawain* and *certain*. In line after line, however, the translation preserves the essential texture of the original. If the alliterative line seems unfamiliar to the eyes of modern readers, we need to remember that the appearance on the page is deceptive because it is visual, not aural. The lines need to be heard. Follow the poet's advice—"If you will listen to this lay . . . I shall tell it . . . With tongue"—and read it aloud. You will find the cadences familiar after all.

Compared with other poems in the Alliterative Revival, *Sir Gawain* shows a remarkably cavalier attitude toward the conventions of the alliterative line. Perhaps chief among these is the prohibition against alliteration on the final stressed syllable; yet we see an example with *one foot further* in the passage above, and there are many more such liberties. As mentioned earlier, some lines pile up more alliterative sounds than the three required in a conventional line, while others lack alliteration altogether. Even the hero's name seems unstable; it is occasionally spelled *Wawain* and alliterates on *w*. Why this looseness? We can reject the idea that the poet lacked adequate control of his medium and wrote shabby lines because of inferior skills. Quite the opposite. The poem *Pearl* in the same manuscript is a masterpiece of versecraft, perhaps unequalled in all of English literature. Written in twelve-lines stanzas with precise alliteration and a demanding rhyme scheme (*a-b-a-b-a-b-a-b-b-c-b-c*), it repeats a key word at the first and last line of each stanza within a section; it has still other exacting formal features. Clearly the poet who wrote *Pearl* could adhere to the comparatively slight demands of the alliterative line in *Gawain*. It is as if in turning to *Sir Gawain* the poet says with a wink, "Let's loosen things up." Because poetic form, far from being mere window-dressing, serves to shape interpretation, *Sir Gawain's* verse form sends a message that is full of energy, is somewhat whimsical, does not take itself too seriously, and toys with conventions without undermining them. It inserts itself into the alliterative tradition in a self-conscious, self-confident way.

This calculated looseness should not be taken to mean that the poem lacks formal control. Evidence of careful design is everywhere. In broad terms *Sir Gawain and the Green Knight* consists of 101 stanzas of varying length, most of which are between twenty and thirty lines including the bob and wheel. The manuscript divides the narrative into four sections of uneven length:

(I)   lines 1 to 490, the initial challenge up to the end of the first year;

(II)   491 to 1125, Gawain's journey and arrival at Hautdesert;

(III)   1126 to 1997, the hunting and bedroom scenes; and

(IV)   1998 to 2530, the episode at the Green Chapel and denouement.

In addition to these broad divisions, still other formal features show the hand of a poet sure of his narrative skills: repeated images, parallel scenes, numerical patternings, rich symbols, character development, and more. Because of this depth the poem has always provided fertile ground for literary close readings — which brings us from the poet as a master of versecraft to the poet as a master story-teller.

Genre and Sources

In creating *Sir Gawain and the Green Knight*, the poet turned to what was by the fourteenth century a shopworn genre in England. The high point of Arthurian romance came two centuries earlier, when Chrétien de Troyes and other authors swept onto the scene with the most innovative form of vernacular literature in Europe. They did so by yoking together the stories of Arthur and his court with the sensibility now known as courtly love or *fin'amor*. Along with amorous idolization, the ethos of courtly love exalted the importance of a knight's honor and chivalrous code of conduct. That Chrétien and others wrote in French was no obstacle to the genre's reception in England, where educated persons above a certain rung on the social ladder, from wealthy merchants to nobility, could be expected to have some command of the language. Over time the freshness of Arthurian romance subsided, and other genres began to take its place. Yet it never disappeared altogether (and aspects persist even today). Some of Chaucer's works incorporate the conventions of courtly love, for example in *Troilus and Criseyde* and *The Knight's Tale*, but it is telling that in *The Canterbury Tales*—and indeed in all of his works—the only Arthurian romance is the tale assigned to the Wife of Bath. However, even if poets rarely cultivated the genre in fourteenth-century England, an impressive number of manuscripts with older French Arthurian romances were owned by Englishmen. Two hundred years after Chrétien, "French Arthurian romances were still being read in bulk in England. . . . [They were] quite simply the most popular form of literary entertainment in the higher strata of society" (Putter 1995, 2).

When the *Gawain*-poet takes up the genre, it is old, familiar, and somewhat nostalgic. As an author his challenge is to breathe life back into it. The first two stanzas give a synopsis of the historical genealogy of Arthur going back to Brutus and Troy, and the poem's final stanza circles back the same history, gesturing to "the best book of romance" and the "Brutus books" (2521, 2523) to lend ancient authority to the tale. This gesture to written authority (often an empty gesture, as here) is itself a time-honored convention, but in fact there are no known sources for the complete *Sir Gawain*. The poet took traditional materials and reworked them into a poem that resembles nothing else that comes before it.

The beheading scene, or more precisely the exchange of blows—a theme well-attested in folklore—seems to go back ultimately to a Celtic source, but the *Gawain*-poet most likely encountered it in *Le Livre de Caradoc*, which forms part of the First Continuation of Chrétien's *Perceval*, which as with other French romances remained popular in England (Benson 1965, 16). What is most remarkable, however, are the systematic changes that the *Gawain*-poet makes to this source, so that little other than the basic framework of the exchange of blows remains. Even a quick glance at similar parts of *Caradoc and Sir Gawain* is enough to reveal the profound transformation.

On the other hand, the temptation scenes, the hunting scenes, and the exchange of winnings motif are less clearly dependent on any sources known to us. Even if there were sources now lost, it seems certain that the *Gawain*-poet reworked them as thoroughly for his purposes as he did *Caradoc*. Most significantly, he transforms each of these traditional sources or themes as he weaves them into a unified story in the service of a guiding artistic vision.

For example, the opening two-stanza prologue emphasizes the chronological distance between the reader and Camelot. One way this is achieved is by making Arthur and his contemporaries child-like as they enjoy the innocent pleasures of their Yule festivities. Arthur is "youthful" and "juvenile" with "young blood"; and upon surveying the court, the Green Knight insults Arthur and his knights by calling them "beardless children." This emphasis on human youthfulness superimposed on the chronological distance of Camelot reinforces the narrator's judgment that "this fair folk" was "in their first age," an age that, however noble and chivalric, is also naive in its remote innocence. The poet's or the reader's society, by contrast, may be older and wiser, but such experience comes at the cost of skepticism about the noblest human ideals. The important point, however, is that these details reveal the imaginative power of the Gawain-poet in manipulating traditional material. There is nothing like it in *Caradoc*.

Narrative Technique

The best way to introduce the poem's narrative technique is to plunge into a sample passage. In the beheading scene at the Chapel, the Green Knight makes two feints with his ax before delivering a "snick" on Gawain's neck. Upon seeing drops of his blood fall on the snow, Gawain springs away and turns in vigorous challenge, assuming a fighting stance. The Green Knight will have none of it, as is clear from what today we would call his body language:

The horseman held himself back,   and on his ax rested,
Set the shaft upon shore,   and on the sharp leaned,

And looked to the liegeman   that on the land went
How that doughty, dreadless,   dauntless there stands
Armed, full fearless: in heart it pleases him.   (2331–35)

The visual contrast of Bertilak's leaning on his ax while looking with amused detachment at Gawain braced for a fight says more about their respective attitudes than dozens of lines of description possibly could. On the one side is a display of valor appropriate to an Arthurian knight, on the other a posture that is indifferent to that valor. The grisly ax becomes a prop for relaxation. Like a painting in two panels, the two images perform an important narrative function, because now the reader's point of view begins to align with Bertilak's. Up to this point the narrative has privileged Gawain's experiences, his adherence to the chivalric code. But Bertilak's relaxed pose subtly draws the reader away from Gawain's perspective, especially after the potentially comic preparation to fight (he broad-jumps and claps his helmet on his head); yet Gawain's reaction "pleases" the reader "in heart" as it does Bertilak. Despite the distancing, despite the fact that the poem does not simply celebrate chivalric ideals as would, say, a French romance from an earlier generation, the reader can nevertheless admire Gawain for his chivalry. To describe this complex yet deft narrative balancing act, Benson makes a useful distinction between unromantic and antiromantic sympathies (Benson 1965, 243). An antiromantic narrative criticizes the unrealistic ideals of pure romance, where rigid adherence to an idealized code of honor leads to self-destruction, as it does eventually to the entire Round Table. The unromantic merely adopts a point of view outside the romance's frame of reference and accepts it as a literary convention. It says that romance is not to be mistaken for reality. Bertilak admires

Gawain for the reasons that the poem's readers have always done, but he holds back, leaning on his ax as he watches the action unfold, as if he were a character who can shift to a position outside of the romance genre. At this point it is as though he is in the romance but not of the romance.

This dichotomy between Bertilak's detachment and Gawain's earnestness continues in the following scene, when Bertilak reveals his admiration for Gawain's exemplary character: compared with other knights he is like a pearl among white peas. But he "lacked a little" in upholding his oath, because he took the girdle. Gawain responds with an outburst condemning himself for cowardice, covetousness, and falseness. What is Bertilak's response to Gawain's self-condemnation? He laughs "lovingly." In other words, Bertilak's laughter does not spring from mockery or contempt but rather from a generosity of spirit because he can see beyond Gawain's horizons of romance, or he finds himself on the outside looking in. Gawain's earnest confession may be appropriate for a knight upholding the absolute ideals of chivalry, but from Bertilak's unromantic point of view those ideals remain out of reach to fallible humans and so excessive that they can seem comic.

The diptych of the Green Knight leaning on his ax and Gawain braced to fight is but one example of the poet's characteristic and pervasive use of concrete visual images. It is not the only such image from this scene, because Gawain leaps away only after seeing his blood shoot to the earth, where it lies in "bright" contrast to the snow on the ground (2314–15). For him, the red blood on white snow is a sign of life. An attentive reader might also be reminded of parallels to the Lady's complexion "Both white and red in blend" (1205) when she first visits him in bed, or even the Green Knight's red eyes (303) as he surveys Arthur's court. Elsewhere, the detailed description of slaughtering and dressing the slain deer, for example, seems to relish visual detail for its own sake. Such emphasis on the concrete creates a sense of realism, making Gawain's blood and the deer's carcass each within imaginative grasp.

The poem's expert use of visual detail contributes to the psychological portrayal of character. For the most part the narrative does not disclose the thoughts and emotions of Gawain or other characters via an omniscient narrator, yet there is no doubt about Gawain's terror when he hears the loud noise of the grindstone sharpening the Green Knight's ax, or his confusion when Lady Bertilak first approaches him in bed, because the concrete descriptions shade toward his point of view.

Another measure of the poem's careful construction are the various symmetries built in to the narrative. Parallels abound: two castles and two courts, two beheading scenes, two confession scenes, a double identity for the Green Knight/Bertilak, and more. The three-part parallels are less frequent, but no less significant. Each of the three hunting scenes is interrupted by the bedroom scene of Lady Bertilak's morning visits to Gawain, where (in a brilliant piece of narrative patterning) she is the hunter and he is her quarry. Even at a level as small as the verse line, the first half balances the second, linked by alliteration; and the syntax often works by juxtaposing one clause with another, which allows the reader to interpret what the pairing means. The poem's architectural symmetry is pervasive, from the smallest detail to the largest elements of structure.

The poem is no less rich in symbolism, even if the values symbolized are often ambiguous. A partial list would include the intruding knight's green color, the holly sprig he carries, the pentangle on Gawain's shield (with its elaborate description), the animals hunted, the tumulus "chapel," and the winter season — including the winter solstice, snow, the feast of Christmas, and New Year's day. Might the snow, for example, signify innocence in its blankness? Or cold sterility? Or seasonal death? Or instead of death, does it become a sign of a fresh start in life, not unlike baptism, after Gawain's blood hits it? Does it signify the soul's purity after confession? The green girdle is richly malleable in what it signifies, because Lady Bertilak, the Green Knight, Gawain, and the Arthurian court each ascribe different values to it at different times. And the meaning ascribed is a sure indication of the lesson drawn from Gawain's adventures by each interpreter.

Themes

As an Arthurian romance, the core themes revolve around Gawain's reputation as a lover and as a fighter; the former is measured by his courtesy and the latter by his bravery. Today (not the fourteenth century) both aspects of the romance hero are conveyed by the term "chivalry." On two occasions Gawain's public reputation for chivalry is called into question. Although both are delivered in mock-seriousness, the accusation stings. "But that ye be Gawain," accuses the Lady at the end of their first interview in the bedroom, "it goes against what I know." (1293; similarly 1481) The real Gawain, the Gawain known through old romances, would not part company after spending so much time with a lady without craving a kiss "by his courtesy." He apologizes, they kiss, and the game of exchanging kisses begins. "Thou art not Gawain," accuses the Green Knight after Gawain flinches when the ax first comes down, because his courage has failed him: "thou fleest for fear ere thou feel harms!" (2270, 2272) These two accusations strike at the core of Gawain's public reputation as a lover and a fighter, although each is less a serious accusation than a rhetorical ploy calculated to manipulate him.

What ultimately motivates Gawain's reputation as a lover and a fighter is a sense of honor, or its more tangible manifestation known as *trawþe* in the original, which is here translated as *troth*. The word's meaning in the fourteenth century has the practical connotations of keeping one's word in society; it is both personal and public, yet the public aspect is indispensable (Green 1999). It is important to bear this in mind, because today "honor" can seem more of an abstraction, like an inner virtue somehow nurtured outside of public view, or like funds kept in a bank account ready for occasional withdrawals. In an Arthurian romance honor is nothing if it is not public; it is nothing if it is not displayed in action. After he is beheaded in Camelot, the Green Knight enjoins Gawain to seek him out in a year and a day *bi þi trawþe*, in the words of the original, and Gawain answers that he will, *by my seker traweþ*, "by my sure troth." As important as it is that Gawain stakes his personal reputation on keeping his word, it is just as important that he declares it in a public setting. Later in the story, when the guide tries to dissuade Gawain from completing his quest at the green chapel, part of the shame of turning away would be the very unpublic nature of such a dishonorable course of action.

Honor, courtesy, and bravery are staples of almost any romance. Another prevalent theme in *Sir Gawain* involves game-playing. In any game, whether it is tic-tac-toe or the most complex roleplaying game, the participants agree to abide by a set of rules that guides their actions. It is limited in having a beginning and an end, and its rules are typically separate from the usual rules of conduct in society. Unless something is amiss, people know when they are engaging in a game and when they are not, and playing it should give pleasure. Some games can be spontaneous, such as the exchange of blows proposed by the Green Knight on New Year's Day in Camelot. Before Gawain swings the ax, he swears to abide by the agreement which, despite its formal language of "troth" and the like, is essentially a game. The pleasure derived from decapitating a giant may be doubtful; the onlookers in Camelot seemed stunned—what kind of game is this?—which is one reason that no knight accepts the challenge at first. Fear is another. But once shamed into action, first Arthur and then Gawain accept the challenge because the return blow seems highly unlikely; from Gawain's perspective, how can he fail to win? Another spontaneous game is the exchange of winnings between Bertilak and Gawain. This one, by contrast, seems like frivolous fun, as host and guest publicly and ceremoniously exchange their winnings at the end of each day—such as three kisses for a fox skin—with much laughter. Its non-serious nature allows Gawain to convince himself to accept and conceal the green girdle in breach of the game's rules. After all, it's just a game. Yet these two games compose the plot of a poem with few peers: *Sir Gawain and the Green Knight*.

Select Bibliography

Verse translations

Armitage, Simon, trans. *Sir Gawain and the Green Knight: A New Verse Translation*. 1st American ed. New York: W.W. Norton, 2007.

Borroff, Marie, trans. *Sir Gawain and the Green Knight. A New Verse Translation*. 1st ed. New York: Norton, 1967.

Merwin, W. S., trans. *Sir Gawain and the Green Knight: A New Verse Translation*. 1st ed. New York: Knopf, 2002.

O'Donoghue, Bernard, trans. *Sir Gawain and the Green Knight*, Penguin Classics. London: Penguin, 2006.

Tolkien, J. R. R., trans. *Sir Gawain and the Green Knight, Pearl*, and *Sir Orfeo*. 1st American ed. Boston: Houghton Mifflin, 1975.

Critical Studies

Benson, Larry Dean. *Art and Tradition in Sir Gawain and the Green Knight*. New Brunswick, NJ: Rutgers University Press, 1965.

Borroff, Marie. *Sir Gawain and the Green Knight: A Stylistic and Metrical Study*, Yale Studies in English, V. 152. New Haven: Yale University Press, 1962.

Borroff, Marie, and Laura L. Howes, edd. *Sir Gawain and the Green Knight: An Authoritative Translation, Contexts, Criticism*. 1st ed, Norton Critical Edition. New York: W.W. Norton, 2010.

Green, Richard Firth. *A Crisis of Truth: Literature and Law in Ricardian England*, The Middle Ages Series. Philadelphia: University of Pennsylvania Press, 1999.

Hanna, Ralph, III. "Unlocking What's Locked: Gawain's Green Girdle." *Viator: Medieval and Renaissance Studies* 14 (1983): 289-302.

Heng, Geraldine. "A Woman Wants: The Lady, Gawain, and the Forms of Seduction." *The Yale Journal of Criticism: Interpretation in the Humanities* 5, no. 3 (1992): 101-34.

Mann, Jill. "Courtly Aesthetics and Courtly Ethics in *Sir Gawain and the Green Knight*." *Studies in the Age of Chaucer: The Yearbook of the New Chaucer Society 31* (2009): 231-65.

Putter, Ad. *Sir Gawain and the Green Knight and French Arthurian Romance.* Oxford: Clarendon Press; New York: Oxford University Press, 1995.

Spearing, A. C. *The Gawain-Poet; a Critical Study.* Cambridge [Eng.]: University Press, 1970.

Staley, Lynn. *The Voice of the Gawain-Poet.* Madison: University of Wisconsin Press, 1984.

Stanbury, Sarah. *Seeing the Gawain-Poet: Description and the Act of Perception,* Middle Ages Series. Philadelphia: University of Pennsylvania Press, 1991.

Editions

Andrew, Malcolm, and R. A. Waldron, edd. *The Poems of the Pearl Manuscript: Pearl, Cleanness, Patience and Sir Gawain and the Green Knight.* 5th ed., Exeter Medieval English Texts and Studies. Exeter: University of Exeter Press, 2007.

Tolkien, J. R. R., E. V. Gordon, and Norman Davis, ed. *Sir Gawain and the Green Knight.* 2nd ed. Oxford: Clarendon Press, 1967.

A Note on the Middle English Original Text

The Middle English text, edited by Donoghue, accepts for the most part the emendations found in Davis's revision of Gordon and Tolkien's edition (1967), with the following exceptions: *Ticius* (11), *glaumande* (line 46), *cayreʒ* (734), *nyʒt* (929), *ʒif* (2343). It retains the letter yogh <ʒ> from the manuscript in word-final position when it conveys the sound [z], as in *cayreʒ*. Punctuation, capitalization, and word division have been changed throughout. The format of the alliterative lines follows the manuscript in leaving the mid-line caesura unmarked even though the rhythm of each line consistently breaks into two halves; the translation, however, indicates the caesura with a space as an aid to the reader.

Sir Gawain and the Green Knight

I

The Middle English Original

1   Siþen þe sege and þe assaut watȝ sesed at Troye,
     Þe borȝ brittened and brent to brondeȝ and askeȝ,
     Þe tulk þat þe trammes of tresoun þer wroȝt
     Watȝ tried for his tricherie, þe trewest on erþe.
5   Hit watȝ Ennias þe athel, and his highe kynde,
     Þat siþen depreced prouinces, and patrounes bicome
     Wel neȝe of al þe wele in þe West Iles.
     Fro riche Romulus to Rome ricchis hym swyþe,
     With gret bobbaunce þat burȝe he biges vpon fyrst,
10   And neuenes hit his aune nome, as hit now hat;
     Ticius to Tuskan and teldes bigynnes,
     Langaberde in Lumbardie lyftes vp homes,
     And fer ouer þe French flod Felix Brutus
     On mony bonkkes ful brode Bretayn he setteȝ
15   wyth wynne,
       Where werre and wrake and wonder
       Bi syþeȝ hatȝ wont þerinne,
       And oft boþe blysse and blunder
       Ful skete hatȝ skyfted synne.

20   Ande quen þis Bretayn watȝ bigged bi þis burn rych,
     Bolde bredden þerinne—baret þat lofden—
     In mony turned tyme tene þat wroȝten.
     Mo ferlyes on þis folde han fallen here oft
     Þen in any oþer þat I wot, syn þat ilk tyme.
25   Bot of alle þat here bult, of Bretaygne kynges,
     Ay watȝ Arthur þe hendest, as I haf herde telle.
     Forþi an aunter in erde I attle to schawe,

The Modern English Translation

1 Once the siege and assault had ceased at Troy,
The burg battered and burned to brands and ashes,
The trooper that the tricks of treason there wrought
Was tried for his treachery, the truest on earth.
5 It was Aeneas the noble and his high-born kin
Who then despoiled provinces and patrons became
Well nigh of all the wealth of the West Isles.
Then rich Romulus to Rome rushes him swiftly,
With great splendor that burg he builds at first,
10 And names it his own name, as it now has.
Ticius to Tuscany and towns he builds;
Longabeard in Lombardy lifts up homes;
And far over the French Flood Felix Brutus
On many banks full broad Britain he sets
15   To begin.
 Where war and wrack and wonder
 Have often flourished there-in,
 And oft both bliss and blunder
 Have ruled in turn since then.

20 And when this Britain was built by this brave knight
Bold men bred there-in— battles they loved—
Who in many a turbulent time troubles have wrought.
More wonders on this field have befallen here oft
Than on any other that I know since that noble time.
25 But of all that here built of British kings
Ever was Arthur the most elegant, as I have heard tell.
Therefore an earthly adventure I aim to show,

3

Þat a selly in siȝt summe men hit holden,
And an outtrage awenture of Arthureȝ wondereȝ.
30   If ȝe wyl lysten þis laye bot on littel quile,
I schal telle hit as-tit, as I in toun herde,
        with tonge,
     As hit is stad and stoken
     In stori stif and stronge,
35   With lel letteres loken,
     In londe so hatȝ ben longe.

Þis kyng lay at Camylot vpon Krystmasse
With mony luflych lorde, ledeȝ of þe best,
Rekenly of þe Rounde Table alle þo rich breþer,
40   With rych reuel oryȝt and rechles merþes.
Þer tournayed tulkes by tymeȝ ful mony,
Justed ful jolilé þise gentyle kniȝtes,
Syþen kayred to þe court caroles to make.
For þer þe fest watȝ ilyche ful fiften dayes,
45   With alle þe mete and þe mirþe þat men couþe avyse;
Such glaumande gle glorious to here,
Dere dyn vpon day, daunsyng on nyȝtes,
Al watȝ hap vpon heȝe in halleȝ and chambreȝ
With lordeȝ and ladies, as leuest him þoȝt.
50   With all þe wele of þe worlde þay woned þer samen,
Þe most kyd knyȝteȝ vnder Krystes seluen,
And þe louelokkest ladies þat euer lif haden,
And he þe comlokest kyng þat þe court haldes;
For al watȝ þis fayre folk in her first age,
55   on sille,
     Þe hapnest vnder heuen,
     Kyng hyȝest mon of wylle;

That a strange sight   some men it hold,

And an awesome adventure   of Arthur's wonders.

30   If you will listen to this lay   but a little while

I shall tell it at once,   as I in town heard

        With tongue,

     As it is set down and struck

     In story stout and strong.

35   With true letters interlocked

     In this land as has been long.

This king lay at Camelot   upon Christmas time

With many loyal lords,   lads of the best,

Renowned of the Round Table   all those rich brethren,

40   With rich revel aright   and reckless mirth.

There tourneyed troopers   by times full many,

Jousted full jollily   these gentle knights,

Then came to the court   carols to make,

For there the feasting was the same   for a full fifteen days

45   With all the meals and the mirth   that man could devise;

Such gladness and glee   glorious to hear,

Dear din upon day,   dancing at night;

All was happiness on high   in halls and chambers,

With lords and ladies,   and most lovely it seemed.

50   With all the wealth of the world   they dwelt there together,

The best known knights   under Christ Himself,

And the loveliest ladies   that ever life had,

And he the comeliest king   that the court holds;

For all was this fair folk   in their first age,

55   And still

     The most fortunate known to fame,

     The king highest man of will.

Hit were now gret nye to neuen
So hardy a here on hille.

60 Wyle Nw ȝer watȝ so ȝep þat hit watȝ nwe cummen,
    Þat day doubble on þe dece watȝ þe douth serued,
    Fro þe kyng watȝ cummen with knyȝtes into þe halle,
    Þe chauntré of þe chapel cheued to an ende.
    Loude crye watȝ þer kest of clerkeȝ and oþer,
65 "Nowel" nayted onewe, neuened ful ofte;
    And syþen riche forth runnen to reche hondeselle,
    Ȝeȝed "Ȝeres-ȝiftes!" on hiȝ, ȝelde hem bi hond,
    Debated busyly aboute þo giftes;
    Ladies laȝed ful loude, þoȝ þay lost haden,
70 And he þat wan watȝ not wrothe, þat may ȝe wel trawe.
    Alle þis mirþe þay maden to þe mete tyme.
    When þay had waschen worþyly þay wenten to sete,
    Þe best burne ay abof, as hit best semed;
    Whene Guenore, ful gay, grayþed in þe myddes,
75 Dressed on þe dere des, dubbed al aboute,
    Smal sendal bisides, a selure hir ouer
    Of tryed tolouse, and tars tapites innoghe,
    Þat were enbrawded and beten wyth þe best gemmes
    Þat myȝt be preued of prys wyth penyes to bye,
80   in daye.
        Þe comlokest to discrye
        Þer glent with yȝen gray;
        A semloker þat euer he syȝe
        Soth moȝt no mon say.

It would now be hard to name
So hardy a host on hill.

60   While New Year was so young,   since it was newly come,
That day with double portions   were the diners served,
For the king was come   with knights into the hall,
The chanting in the chapel   achieved an end.
Loud cries were there cast   by clerics and others,
65   "Noel" named anew,   announced full oft;
And then the rich run forth   to render presents
Yelled "Year's gifts!" on high,   yielding them by hand,
Debated busily   about those gifts;
Ladies laughed full loud,   though they had lost,
70   And he that won was not wroth,   that may you well believe.
All this mirth they made   until the meal time.
When they had washed worthily,   they went to sit,
The best brave always above,   as it best seemed;
Queen Guenevere, full gay,   graced the middle,
75   Bedecked on the dear dais,   adorned all about,
Fine silk at her sides,   a ceiling above
Of rich cloth of Toulouse,   and of Tartary many tapestries
Embroidered and bedecked   with the best gems
That might be proven in price   with pounds to buy
80   In our day.
      The comeliest to see
      There gleamed with eyes of gray;
      A fairer that ever could be
      In sooth might no man say.

7

85   Bot Arthure wolde not ete til al were serued,
      He watȝ so joly of his joyfnes, and sumquat childgered:
      His lif liked hym lyȝt; he louied þe lasse
      Auþer to longe lye or to longe sitte,
      So bisied him his ȝonge blod and his brayn wylde.
90   And also an oþer maner meued him eke
      Þat he þurȝ nobelay had nomen: he wolde neuer ete
      Vpon such a dere day er hym deuised were
      Of sum auenturus þyng, an vncouþe tale,
      Of sum mayn meruayle þat he myȝt trawe,
95   Of alderes, of armes, of oþer auenturus,
      Oþer sum segg hym bisoȝt of sum siker knyȝt
      To joyne wyth hym in iustyng, in jopardé to lay
      Lede lif for lyf, leue vchon oþer
      As fortune wolde fulsun hom, þe fayrer to haue.
100   Þis watȝ þe kynges countenaunce where he in court were,
      At vch farand fest among his fre meny
                in halle.
            Þerfore of face so fere
            He stiȝtleȝ stif in stalle.
105   Ful ȝep in þat Nw ȝere
            Much mirthe he mas withalle.

      Thus þer stondes in stale þe stif kyng hisseluen,
      Talkkande bifore þe hyȝe table of trifles ful hende.
      There gode Gawan watȝ grayþed Gwenore bisyde,
110   And Agrauayn a la Dure Mayn on þat oþer syde sittes,
      Boþe þe kynges sistersunes and ful siker kniȝtes.
      Bischop Bawdewyn abof bigineȝ þe table,
      And Ywan, Vryn son, ette with hymseluen.

8

85	But Arthur would not eat until all were served,
	He was so jolly and joyful, and somewhat juvenile:
	He liked his life light; he loved least
	Either too long to lie or too long to sit
	So busied him his young blood and his brain wild.
90	And also another matter moved him as well,
	That he had adopted for nobility: he would never eat
	Upon such a dear day ere he was told
	Of some adventurous thing, an astonishing tale
	Of some mighty marvel that he might believe
95	Of our elders, of arms, of other adventures,
	Or some stalwart besought him for some true knight
	To join with him in jousting, in jeopardy to lay
	At risk life for life, each happy if the other
	By Fortune was favored the advantage to have.
100	This was the king's custom whenever he was in court
	At each fine feast among his fair retinue
	In hall.
	Therefore of face so fair
	He stands strong at his stall.
105	Full youthful in that New Year,
	Much mirth he makes with all.

	Thus there stands at his stall the strong king himself,
	Talking before the high table of trifles full courtly.
	There good Gawain was seated Guenevere beside,
110	And Agravain of the Hard Hand on that other side sits,
	Both the king's sister's sons and full sure knights.
	Bishop Baldwin above begins the table
	And Ywain, Urien's son, ate with Arthur himself.

Þise were diȝt on þe des and derworþly serued,

115 And siþen mony siker segge at þe sidbordeȝ.

Þen þe first cors come with crakkyng of trumpes,

Wyth mony baner ful bryȝt þat þerbi henged;

Nwe nakryn noyse with þe noble pipes,

Wylde werbles and wyȝt wakned lote,

120 Þat mony hert ful hiȝe hef at her towches.

Dayntés dryuen þerwyth of ful dere metes,

Foysoun of þe fresche, and on so fele disches

Þat pine to fynde þe place þe peple biforne

For to sette þe sylueren þat sere sewes halden

125   on clothe.

       Iche lede as he loued hymselue

       Þer laȝt withouten loþe;

       Ay two had disches twelue,

       Good ber and bryȝt wyn boþe.

130 Now wyl I of hor seruise say yow no more,

For vch wyȝe may wel wit no wont þat þer were.

An oþer noyse ful newe neȝed biliue,

Þat þe lude myȝt haf leue liflode to cach;

For vneþe watȝ þe noyce not a whyle sesed,

135 And þe fyrst cource in þe court kyndely serued,

Þer hales in at þe halle dor an aghlich mayster,

On þe most on þe molde on mesure hyghe,

Fro þe swyre to þe swange so sware and so þik,

And his lyndes and his lymes so longe and so grete,

140 Half etayn in erde I hope þat he were;

Bot mon most I algate mynn hym to bene,

And þat þe myriest in his muckel þat myȝt ride,

For of bak and of brest al were his bodi sturne,

10

These were dining on the dais,   diligently served,

115   And next were many sure stalwarts   at the sideboards.
Then the first course came   with cracking of trumpets
With many banners full bright   that there-by hung;
New noise of drums   with the noble pipes,
Wild warbles and loud   wakened echoes,

120   That many hearts heaved   full high at their notes.
Dainties drummed in there-with   of many dear foods,
Full plenty of fresh food   and on so many fair dishes
That it was a pain to find place   the people before
To set the silver that held   the separate stews

125   On cloth.
Each lad as he loved himself
There dined, nothing loath;
Each two had dishes twelve,
Good beer and bright wine both.

130   Now will I of their service   say you no more,
For each warrior may well know   no want was there.
Another noise full new   quickly came nigh
That the lord might have leave   to lift up his food,
For hardly was the noise   not a while ceased,

135   And the first course in the court   courteously served,
There hastens in at the hall door   an awesome figure,
One of the most on earth   in measure of height,
From the neck to the waist   so well-built and square,
And his loins and his limbs   so long and so big

140   Half a giant in earth   I affirm that he was;
Yet man must I nonetheless   admit him to be
And that the merriest in his muchness   that might ride,
For though of back and of breast   his body was stout,

Both his wombe and his wast were worthily smale,
145   And alle his fetures folyande, in forme þat he hade,
            ful clene;
        For wonder of his hwe men hade,
        Set in his semblaunt sene:
        He ferde as freke were fade,
150   And oueral enker grene.

        Ande al grayþed in grene þis gome and his wedes:
        A strayte cote ful streȝt, þat stek on his sides,
        A meré mantile abof, mensked withinne
        With pelure pured apert, þe pane ful clene
155   With blyþe blaunner ful bryȝt, and his hod boþe,
        Þat watȝ laȝt fro his lokkeȝ and layde on his schulderes;
        Heme wel-haled hose of þat same,
        Þat spenet on his sparlyr, and clene spures vnder
        Of bryȝt golde, vpon silk bordes barred ful ryche,
160   And scholes vnder schankes þere þe schalk rides,
        And alle his vesture uerayly watȝ clene verdure,
        Boþe þe barres of his belt and oþer blyþe stones,
        Þat were richely rayled in his aray clene
        Aboutte hymself and his sadel, vpon silk werkeȝ.
165   Þat were to tor for to telle of tryfles þe halue
        Þat were enbrauded abof, wyth bryddes and flyȝes,
        With gay gaudi of grene, þe golde ay inmyddes,
        Þe pendauntes of his payttrure, þe proude cropure;
        His molaynes, and alle þe metail anamayld was þenne,
170   Þe steropes þat he stod on stayned of þe same,
        And his arsounȝ al after and his aþel skyrtes,
        Þat euer glemered and glent al of grene stones.

12

Both his belly and his waist   were worthily slim,
145   And all his features conforming,   in form that he had,
            Full clean.
        But great wonder of the hue men had
        Set in his complexion seen:
        He fared like a fighter to dread,
150   And over all deep green.

And all garbed in green   this gallant and his clothes:
A straight coat full tight   that stuck to his sides,
A merry mantle above,   embellished within
With finely trimmed furs,   a facing full bright
155   Of handsome white ermine   and his hood as well,
That was lifted from his locks   and laid on his shoulders;
Neat well-fitting hose   of that same green
That covered his calves,   and shining spurs below
Of bright gold, on silken borders   embroidered full rich,
160   And with fine shoes below the shanks   the chevalier rides,
And all his vesture verily   was verdant green,
Both the bars of his belt   and other bright stones,
That were richly arranged   in his array completely
About himself and his saddle,   upon silk works
165   That would be too toilsome to tell   of trifles the half
That were embroidered above,   with insects, and birds
With gay gems of green,   and gold intermingled,
The pendants of his horse trappings,   the proud crupper;
His mount's bit and all the metal   enamelled was then,
170   The stirrups that he stood on   colored the same,
And his saddle-bow next   and its elegant skirts
That ever glimmered and glowed   all of green stones.

Þe fole þat he ferkkes on fyn of þat ilke,
       sertayn:

175   A grene hors gret and þikke,
       A stede ful stif to strayne;
       In brawden brydel quik,
       To þe gome he watȝ ful gayn.

Wel gay watȝ þis gome gered in grene,
180   And þe here of his hed of his hors swete.
Fayre fannand fax vmbefoldes his schulderes,
A much berd as a busk ouer his brest henges
Þat wyth his hiȝlich here þat of his hed reches
Watȝ euesed al vmbetorne abof his elbowes,
185   Þat half his armes þer-vnder were halched in þe wyse
Of a kyngeȝ capados þat closes his swyre;
Þe mane of þat mayn hors much to hit lyke,
Wel cresped and cemmed, wyth knottes ful mony,
Folden in wyth fildore aboute þe fayre grene,
190   Ay a herle of þe here, an oþer of golde,
Þe tayl and his toppyng twynnen of a sute,
And bounden boþe wyth a bande of a bryȝt grene,
Dubbed wyth ful dere stoneȝ, as þe dok lasted,
Syþen þrawen wyth a þwong a þwarle knot alofte,
195   Þer mony belleȝ ful bryȝt of brende golde rungen.
Such a fole vpon folde ne freke þat hym rydes
Watȝ neuer sene in þat sale wyth syȝt er þat tyme
       With yȝe.
       He loked as layt so lyȝt,
200   So sayd al þat hym syȝe;
       Hit semed as no mon myȝt
       Vnder his dyntteȝ dryȝe.

The foal he fares on   fully of that same hue,
        Certain:
        A green horse great and thick,
        A steed full stiff to restrain;
        In embroidered bridle quick,
        For the gallant who held the rein.

Well gay was this gallant   and his gear in green,
And the hair of his head   matching his horse.
Fair fanning locks   enfold his shoulders,
A beard big as a bush   over his breast hangs
That with the noble hair   that from his head reaches
Was clipped all around   above his elbows
That half his arms there-under   were held in the manner
Of a king's cape   that encloses his neck;
The mane of that mighty horse   much to it like,
Well curled and combed   with knots full many,
Tied in with gold thread   about the fair green,
Always one strand of hair,   another of gold,
His tail and his topknot   twisted in braids,
And both bound with a band   of bright green,
Adorned with full dear gems   to the top of the tuft,
Then bound tightly with a thong,   trickily knotted above,
Where many bells full bright   of burnished gold rang.
Such a foal in the field   nor fighter that rides him
Was never seen in that hall   with sight ere that time
        With eye.
        He looked like lightning as light,
        Said all that saw him come nigh;
        It seemed that no man might
        Such blows as his defy.

175

180

185

190

195

200

Wheþer hade he no helme ne hawbergh nauþer,
Ne no pysan ne no plate þat pented to armes,
205   Ne no schafte ne no schelde to schwue ne to smyte,
Bot in his on honde he hade a holyn bobbe,
Þat is grattest in grene when greueȝ ar bare,
And an ax in his oþer, a hoge and vnmete,
A spetos sparþe to expoun in spelle, quoso myȝt.
210   Þe lenkþe of an elnȝerde þe large hede hade,
Þe grayn al of grene stele and of golde hewen.
Þe bit burnyst bryȝt, with a brod egge
As wel schapen to schere as scharp rasores.
Þe stele of a stif staf þe sturne hit bi grypte,
215   Þat watȝ wounden wyth yrn to þe wandeȝ ende,
And al bigrauen with grene in gracios werkes;
A lace lapped aboute, þat louked at þe hede,
And so after þe halme halched ful ofte,
Wyth tryed tasseleȝ þerto tacched innoȝe
220   On botounȝ of þe bryȝt grene brayden ful ryche.
Þis haþel heldeȝ hym in and þe halle entres,
Driuande to þe heȝe dece — dut he no woþe;
Haylsed he neuer one, bot heȝe he ouer loked.
Þe fyrst word þat he warp, "Wher is," he sayd,
225   "Þe gouernour of þis gyng? Gladly I wolde
Se þat segg in syȝt, and with hymself speke
        raysoun."
    To knyȝteȝ he kest his yȝe,
    And reled hym vp and doun;
230   He stemmed, and con studie
    Quo walt þer most renoun.

Yet he had no helmet   nor hauberk neither,

Nor any armor nor plate   that pertained to arms,

205   Nor any spear nor any shield   to shove nor to smite,

But in his one hand   he had a holly branch,

That is greatest in green   when groves are bare,

And an ax in his other,   awesome and monstrous,

A spiteful ax to describe in speech,   if anyone could.

210   Near four feet in length   the large head had,

With a spike of green steel   and of hammered gold.

The bit burnished bright   with a broad edge,

As well shaped to shear   as a sharp razor.

By the hilt of the strong shaft   that stern one it gripped

215   That was wound with iron   to the weapon's end,

And all engraved with green   in gracious works;

By a lace sash, coiled about,   that was tied at the head

And so down the shaft   looped full oft,

With fine tassles there-to   attached there-by,

220   And buttons of bright green,   embroidered full rich.

This horseman held his way in   and the hall enters,

Driving to the high dais—   no danger he feared;

Hailed he never any one   but high he looked over.

The first word that he whipped out: "Where is," he said,

225   "The governor of this gang?   Gladly I would

See that stalwart in sight   and speak with himself

And reason."

To knights he cast his eyes

And rolled them up and down;

230   He stopped and studied to surmise

Who wields there most renown.

Ther watȝ lokyng on lenþe þe lude to beholde,
For vch mon had meruayle quat hit mene myȝt
Þat a haþel and a horse myȝt such a hwe lach.

235 As growe grene as þe gres and grener hit semed,
Þen grene aumayl on golde glowande bryȝter.
Al studied þat þer stod, and stalked hym nerre
Wyth al þe wonder of þe worlde what he worch schulde,
For fele sellyeȝ had þay sen, bot such neuer are;

240 Forþi for fantoum and fayryȝe þe folk þere hit demed.
Þerfore to answare watȝ arȝe mony aþel freke,
And al stouned at his steuen and stonstil seten
In a swoȝe sylence þurȝ þe sale riche;
As al were slypped vpon slepe so slaked hor loteȝ

245   in hyȝe —
        I deme hit not al for doute,
        Bot sum for cortaysye —
        Bot let hym þat al schulde loute
        Cast vnto þat wyȝe.

250 Þenn Arþour bifore þe hiȝ dece þat auenture byholdeȝ,
And rekenly hym reuerenced, for rad was he neuer,
And sayde, "Wyȝe, welcum iwys to þis place;
Þe hede of þis ostel Arthour I hat;
Liȝt luflych adoun and lenge, I þe praye,

255 And quat-so þy wylle is we schal wyt after."
"Nay, as help me," quoþ þe haþel, "he þat on hyȝe syttes,
To wone any quyle in þis won, hit watȝ not myn ernde;
Bot for þe los of þe, lede, is lyft vp so hyȝe,
And þy burȝ and þy burnes best ar holden,

There was looking at length   the liegeman to behold,
For each man had marvel   what it might mean
That a horsemen and a horse   might have such a hue.
235   As green as the growing grass   and greener it seemed
Than green enamel on gold   glowing brighter.
All studied that there stood   and stalked him nearer,
With all the wonder of the world   of what he would do,
For many spectacles had they seen   but such as this never;
240   Thus from fantasy and fairyland   the folk there it deemed.
Therefore to answer were afraid   many elegant fighters,
And all were astounded by his speech,   and sat stone-still
In a swooning dead stillness   through the silent hall,
As if all were slipped into sleep   so slackened their noises
245   On high—
        I deem it not all for fear,
        But some, for courtesy shy,
        Let him whom all should revere
        To that warrior give reply.

250   Then Arthur before the high dais   that adventure beholds
And rightly reverenced him,   for feared was he never,
And said "Warrior,   welcome indeed to this place;
The head of this hostel   Arthur I am called
Light lovely adown   and linger I pray thee
255   And whatever thy will is   we shall know later,"
"Nay, so help me," quoth the horseman,   "He that on high sits,
To dwell any while in this dwelling   was not my errand;
But for the laud of thee, lad,   is lifted up so high,
And thy burg and thy braves   best are held,

260   Stifest vnder stel-gere on stedes to ryde,
      Þe wyȝtest and þe worþyest of þe worldes kynde,
      Preue for to play wyth in oþer pure laykeȝ,
      And here is kydde cortaysye, as I haf herd carp,
      And þat hatȝ wayned me hider, iwyis, at þis tyme.
265   Ȝe may be seker bi þis braunch þat I bere here
      Þat I passe as in pes, and no plyȝt seche,
      For had I founded in fere in feȝtyng wyse,
      I haue a hauberȝe at home and a helme boþe,
      A schelde and a scharp spere, schinande bryȝt,
270   Ande oþer weppenes to welde, I wene wel, als;
      Bot for I wolde no were, my wedeȝ ar softer.
      Bot if þou be so bold as alle burneȝ tellen,
      Þou wyl grant me godly þe gomen þat I ask,
                  bi ryȝt."
275   Arthour con onsware
            And sayd, "Sir cortays knyȝt,
            If þou craue batayl bare,
            Here fayleȝ þou not to fyȝt."

      "Nay, frayst I no fyȝt, in fayth I þe telle.
280   Hit arn aboute on þis bench bot berdleȝ chylder.
      If I were hasped in armes on a heȝe stede,
      Here is no mon me to mach, for myȝteȝ so wayke.
      Forþy I craue in þis court a Crystemas gomen,
      For hit is Ȝol and Nwe Ȝer, and here ar Ȝep mony.
285   If any so hardy in þis hous holdeȝ hymseluen
      Be so bolde in his blod, brayn in hys hede
      Þat dar stifly strike a strok for an oþer
      I schal gif hym of my gyft þys giserne ryche,

260   Stoutest under steel gear   on steeds to ride,
           The strongest and the worthiest   of this world's kind,
           With prowess in jousting   and other pure sports,
           And here is famed courtesy,   as I have heard claimed,
           And that has drawn me here,   indeed, at this time.
265   You may be sure by this branch   that I bear here
           That I pass here in peace   and no peril seek,
           For had I fared here with a force   for fighting ready,
           I have a mail coat at home   and a helmet too,
           A shield and a sharp spear,   shining bright,
270   And other weapons to wield   I know well also;
           But since I want no war,   my weeds are softer.
           But if thou be as bold   as all battlers tell,
           Thou will grant me goodly   the game that I ask,
                By right."
275   Arthur gave answer
                And said, "Sir courteous knight,
                If thou crave battle of armor bare,
                Here failest thou not to fight."

    "Nay, I seek no fight,   in faith I thee tell.
280   Here about on this bench   are but beardless children.
           If I were harnessed in armor   on a high steed
           Here is no man to match me,   their mights are so weak.
           Therefore I crave in this court   a Christmas game,
           For it is Yule and New Year   and here are youths many.
285   If any so hardy in this house   holds himself,
           Or is so bold in his blood,   brain-mad in his head
           That dare stiffly strike   one stroke for another
           I shall give him of my gift   this great battle-ax,

Þis ax, þat is heué innogh, to hondele as hym lykes,

290   And I schal bide þe fyrst bur as bare as I sitte.

If any freke be so felle to fonde þat I telle

Lepe lyȝtly me to, and lach þis weppen;

I quit-clayme hit for euer, kepe hit as his auen,

And I schal stonde hym a strok, stif on þis flet,

295   Elleȝ þou wyl diȝt me þe dom to dele hym an oþer

        barlay—

      And ȝet gif hym respite,

      A twelmonyth and a day.

      Now hyȝe, and let se tite

300   Dar any herinne oȝt say."

If he hem stowned vpon fyrst, stiller were þanne

Alle þe heredmen in halle, þe hyȝ and þe loȝe.

Þe renk on his rouncé hym ruched in his sadel,

And runischly his rede yȝen he reled aboute,

305   Bende his bresed broȝeȝ, blycande grene,

Wayued his berde for to wayte quo-so wolde ryse.

When non wolde kepe hym with carp he coȝed ful hyȝe,

Ande rimed hym ful richly, and ryȝt hym to speke.

"What? Is þis Arthures hous," quoþ þe haþel þenne,

310   "Þat al þe rous rennes of þurȝ ryalmes so mony?

Where is now your sourquydrye and your conquestes,

Your gryndellayk and your greme, and your grete wordes?

Now is þe reuel and þe renoun of þe Rounde Table

Ouerwalt wyth a worde of on wyȝes speche,

315   For al dares for drede withoute dynt schewed!"

Wyth þis he laȝes so loude þat þe lorde greued;

This ax, that is heavy enough,   to handle as he pleases,

290   And I shall abide the first blow   as bare as I sit.

If any fighter be so fierce   to test what I tell

Leap lightly to me   and lay hold of this weapon;

I quit-claim it forever;   let him keep it as his own,

And I shall stand one stroke from him,   stout on this floor,

295   If thou will grant me the right   to render him another.

—Time out today!—

And yet I give him respite,

A twelvemonth and a day.

Now hurry and let's see aright

300   If any dare anything say."

If he astounded them at first,   stiller were then

All the courtiers in the hall,   the high and the low;

The rider on his mount   moved him in his saddle

And roughly his red eyes   he rolled about,

305   Bent his bushy brows   brightly green,

Waved his beard to see   whoever would arise.

When none kept him there with talk,   he coughed "ahem,"

And rose up full lordly   and readied himself to speak.

"What? Is this Arthur's house"   quoth the horseman then,

310   "That all the renown runs   through realms so many?

Where is now your vainglory   and your victories,

Your ferocity and your grimness   and your great words?

Now is the revel and renown   of the Round Table

Overthrown by one word   of one warrior's speech,

315   For all dither for dread   without deed shown!"

With this he laughs so loud   that the lord grieved.

Þe blod schot for scham into his schyre face
    and lere;
    He wex as wroth as wynde,
320   So did alle þat þer were.
    Þe kyng as kene bi kynde
    Þen stod þat stif mon nere,

Ande sayde, "Haþel, by heuen, þyn askyng is nys,
And as þou foly hatȝ frayst, fynde þe behoues.
325   I know no gome þat is gast of þy grete wordes.
Gif me now þy geserne, vpon Godeȝ halue,
And I schal bayþen þy bone þat þou boden habbes."
Lyȝtly lepeȝ he hym to, and laȝt at his honde,
Þen feersly þat oþer freke vpon fote lyȝtis.
330   Now hatȝ Arthure his axe, and þe halme grypeȝ,
And sturnely stureȝ hit aboute, þat stryke wyth hit þoȝt;
Þe stif mon hym bifore stod vpon hyȝt,
Herre þen ani in þe hous by þe hede and more.
Wyth sturne schere þer he stod he stroked his berde,
335   And wyth a countenaunce dryȝe he droȝ doun his cote,
No more mate ne dismayd for hys mayn dinteȝ
Þen any burne vpon bench hade broȝt hym to drynk
    of wyne.
    Gawan, þat sate bi þe quene,
340   To þe kyng he can enclyne:
    "I beseche now with saȝeȝ sene
    Þis melly mot be myne.

"Wolde ȝe, worþilych lorde," quoþ Wawan to þe kyng,
"Bid me boȝe fro þis benche, and stonde by yow þere,

The blood shot for shame   in his shining white face
       So fair;
    He waxed as wroth as wind,
320   So did all that were there.
    The king, as keen by kind
    Then strode that stout man nearer,

And said "Horseman, by heaven,   thine asking is foolish,
And as thou folly hast sought,   to find it thee behooves.
325 I know no gallant that is aghast   of thy great words.
Give me now thy great ax,   by God's wounds,
And I shall bestow the boon   that thou hast begged."
Lightly leaps he him to   and latches it from his hand
Then fiercely that other fighter   upon foot alights.
330 Now has Arthur his ax,   and the hilt grips,
And sternly swings it about,   and meant to strike with it;
The stout man before him   stood up straight,
Higher than any in the house,   by the head and more.
With stern stance where he stood   he stroked his beard,
335 And with a countenance dry   he drew down his coat,
No more moved nor dismayed   for his mighty blows
Than if any battler upon bench   had brought him a drink
       Of wine.
    Gawain, that sat by the queen,
340   To the king he did incline:
    "I beseech now with plain speech
    This melee may be mine.

"Would ye, worthy lord,"   quoth Wawain to the king,
"Bid me bow from this bench   and stand by you there,

345   Þat I wythoute vylanye myȝt voyde þis table,
And þat my legge lady lyked not ille,
I wolde com to your counseyl bifore your cort ryche,
For me þink hit not semly, as hit is soþ knawen,
Þer such an askyng is heuened so hyȝe in your sale,
350   Þaȝ ȝe ȝourself be talenttyf, to take hit to yourseluen,
Whil mony so bolde yow aboute vpon bench sytten,
Þat vnder heuen I hope non haȝerer of wylle,
Ne better bodyes on bent þer baret is rered.
I am þe wakkest, I wot, and of wyt feblest,
355   And lest lur of my lyf, quo laytes þe soþe;
Bot for as much as ȝe ar myn em I am only to prayse;
No bounté bot your blod I in my bodé knowe,
And syþen þis note is so nys þat noȝt hit yow falles,
And I haue frayned hit at yow fyrst, foldeȝ hit to me;
360   And if I carp not comlyly, let alle þis cort rych
        bout blame."
      Ryche togeder con roun,
      And syþen þay redden alle same:
      To ryd þe kyng wyth croun,
365   And gif Gawan þe game.

Þen comaunded þe kyng þe knyȝt for to ryse,
And he ful radly vpros, and ruchched hym fayre,
Kneled doun bifore þe kyng, and cacheȝ þat weppen,
And he luflyly hit hym laft, and lyfte vp his honde,
370   And gef hym Goddeȝ blessyng, and gladly hym biddes
Þat his hert and his honde schulde hardi be boþe.
"Kepe þe, cosyn," quoþ þe kyng, "þat þou on kyrf sette.
And if þou redeȝ hym ryȝt, redly I trowe
Þat þou schal byden þe bur þat he schal bede after."

345   That I without vile manners   might vacate this table,
           And providing my liege lady   be not ill pleased,
           I would come to your counsel   before your rich court,
           For I think it not seemly,   as it is sooth known
           That such an asking be heaved up   so high in your hall,
350   Though you yourself be tempted   to take it to yourself
           While so many bold about you   upon bench sit
           That under heaven I hold   none hardier of will,
           Nor better bodies on earth   where battle is reared.
           I am the weakest, I know,   and of wit feeblest,
355   And my life would be the least loss,   to speak the sooth,
           For only because you are my uncle   am I to be praised;
           No goodness but your blood   I in my body know,
           And since this business is so foolish,   it does not befit you,
           And I have begged it of you first,   inflict it on me;
360   And if I speak not courteously,   let all this court rich
                    Me blame."
               Rich nobles gathered round
               And they all advised the same:
               To replace the king with crown,
365   And give Gawain the game.

           Then commanded the king   the knight for to rise,
           And he full readily uprose   and arranged himself fairly,
           Kneeled down before the king   and catches that weapon,
           And Arthur lovingly left it to him   and lifted up his hands
370   And gave him God's blessing   and gladly him bids
           That his heart and his hands   should hardy be both.
           "Take care, kinsman," quoth the king,   "that thou cut but once.
           And if thou deal with him rightly,   readily I believe
           Thou shalt survive the blow   he shall bring there-after."

375   Gawan gotȝ to þe gome with giserne in honde,
        And he baldly hym bydeȝ, he bayst neuer þe helder.
        Þen carppeȝ to Sir Gawan þe knyȝt in þe grene,
        "Refourme we oure forwardes, er we fyrre passe.
        Fyrst I eþe þe, haþel, how þat þou hattes;
380   Þat þou me telle truly, as I tryst may."
        "In god fayth," quoþ þe goode knyȝt, "Gawan I hatte,
        Þat bede þe þis buffet, quat-so bifalleȝ after,
        And at þis tyme twelmonyth take at þe an oþer
        Wyth what weppen so þou wylt, and wyth no wyȝ elleȝ
385   on lyue."
          Þat oþer onswareȝ agayn,
          "Sir Gawan, so mot I þryue,
          As I am ferly fayn
          Þis dint þat þou schal dryue.

390   "Bigog!" quoþ þe grene knyȝt, "Sir Gawan, me lykes
        Þat I schal fange at þy fust þat I haf frayst here.
        And þou hatȝ redily rehersed, bi resoun ful trwe,
        Clanly al þe couenaunt þat I þe kynge asked,
        Saf þat þou schal siker me, segge, bi þi trawþe,
395   Þat þou schal seche me þiself, where-so þou hopes
        I may be funde vpon folde, and foch þe such wages
        As þou deles me to-day bifore þis douþe ryche."
        "Where schulde I wale þe," quoþ Gauan, "where is þy place?
        I wot neuer where þou wonyes, bi hym þat me wroȝt,
400   Ne I know not þe, knyȝt, þy cort ne þi name.
        Bot teche me truly þerto, and telle me how þou hattes,
        And I schal ware alle my wyt to wynne me þeder,

375 Gawain goes to the gallant   with the great ax in hand,
And he boldly him abides;   he was abashed not at all.
Then calls out to Sir Gawain   the knight in the green,
"Let us affirm our pledge,   ere we further pace.
First I ask thee, horseman,   how thou art called;
380 That thou tell me truly,   so I can trust."
"In good faith," quoth the good knight,   "Gawain I am called,
Who grants thee this buffet,   whatever after befalls,
And from this time a twelvemonth   I will take one from thee,
With whatever weapon as thou wish   and with no other warrior
385   Alive."
         The other answers again:
         "Sir Gawain, as I may thrive,
         I am greatly glad, certain,
         That thou this blow shalt drive."

390 "By Gog!" quoth the green knight,   "Sir Gawain, I like it
That I shall feel from your fist,   the favor I have asked.
And thou hast readily rehearsed,   by reason full true,
Completely all the covenant   that I of the king asked,
Save that thou shall assure me,   good sir, by thy troth,
395 That thou shall seek me thyself,   wherever thou supposest
I may be found upon earth,   and fetch thee such wages
As thou dealest to me today   before this dear court."
"Where do I find thee?" quoth Gawain,   "where is thy place?
I am not aware where thou dwellest,   by Him that me wrought,
400 Nor I know not thee, knight,   thy court nor thy name.
But teach me truly   and tell me how thou art called,
And I shall work with all my wit   to win my way thither,

And þat I swere þe for soþe, and by my seker traweþ."

"Þat is innogh in Nwe ȝer; hit nedes no more,"

405 Quoþ þe gome in þe grene to Gawan þe hende.

"ȝif I þe telle trwly, quen I þe tape haue

And þou me smoþely hatȝ smyten, smartly I þe teche

Of my hous and my home and myn owen nome,

Þen may þou frayst my fare and forwardeȝ holde;

410 And if I spende no speche, þenne spedeȝ þou þe

better,

For þou may leng in þy londe and layt no fyrre—

bot slokes!

Ta now þy grymme tole to þe,

And let se how þou cnokeȝ."

415 "Gladly, sir, for soþe,"

Quoþ Gawan; his ax he strokes.

Þe grene knyȝt vpon grounde grayþely hym dresses,

A littel lut with þe hede, þe lere he discouereȝ;

His longe louelych lokkeȝ he layd ouer his croun,

420 Let þe naked nec to þe note schewe.

Gauan gripped to his ax, and gederes hit on hyȝt,

Þe kay fot on þe folde he before sette,

Let him doun lyȝtly lyȝt on þe naked,

Þat þe scharp of þe schalk schyndered þe bones,

425 And schrank þurȝ þe schyre grece, and schade hit in twynne,

Þat þe bit of þe broun stel bot on þe grounde.

Þe fayre hede fro þe halce hit to þe erþe,

Þat fele hit foyned wyth her fete, þere hit forth roled.

Þe blod brayd fro þe body, þat blykked on þe grene,

430 And nawþer faltered ne fel þe freke neuer þe helder,

Bot styþly he start forth vpon styf schonkes,

And that I swear thee for sooth   and by my sure troth."
"That is enough in the New Year;   it needs no more,"
405   Quoth the gallant in the green   to Gawain the courtier.
"If I tell thee truly   when I have tapped thee,
And thou me smoothly hast smitten,   smartly I will teach thee
Of my house and my home   and my own name.
Then may thou be my guest   and our agreements fulfill;
410   And if I cannot speak any speech,   then succeedest thou the
                                                      better,
For thou may linger in thy land   and look no farther.
          Thou spokest!
       Take now thy grim tool, in truth,
       And let's see how thou pokest."
415   "Gladly, sir, for sooth,"
       Quoth Gawain; his ax he strokes.

This green knight upon ground   gracefully him readies,
A little bow with his head   the face he uncovers;
His long lovely locks   he laid over his crown
420   Let the naked neck   show to the nape.
Gawain gripped to his ax   and gathers it on high,
The left foot on the floor   he set before,
Let it down swiftly alight   on the naked skin
That the sharp of the chevalier   shattered the bones
425   And sheared through the shining flesh   and slashed it in two,
That the bit of the bright steel   bit on the ground.
The fair head from the neck   hit on the earth,
That full many it kicked with their feet,   where it forth rolled.
The blood poured from the body,   bright on the green,
430   And neither faltered nor fell   the fighter nonetheless,
But stoutly he starts forth   upon strong shanks,

And runyschly he raȝt out, þere as renkkeȝ stoden,
Laȝt to his lufly hed, and lyft hit vp sone;
And syþen boȝeȝ to his blonk, þe brydel he cachcheȝ,
435 Steppeȝ into stelbawe and strydeȝ alofte,
And his hede by þe here in his honde haldeȝ,
And as sadly þe segge hym in his sadel sette
As non vnhap had hym ayled, þaȝ hedleȝ he were
in stedde.
440 He brayde his bulk aboute,
Þat vgly bodi þat bledde;
Moni on of hym had doute,
Bi þat his resounȝ were redde,

For þe hede in his honde he haldeȝ vp euen,
445 Toward þe derrest on þe dece he dresseȝ þe face,
And hit lyfte vp þe yȝe-lyddeȝ and loked ful brode,
And meled þus much with his muthe, as ȝe may now here:
"Loke, Gawan, þou be grayþe to go as þou hetteȝ,
And layte as lelly til þou me, lude, fynde,
450 As þou hatȝ hette in þis halle, herande þise knyȝtes;
To þe grene chapel þou chose, I charge þe, to fotte
Such a dunt as þou hatȝ dalt—disserued þou habbeȝ—
To be ȝederly ȝolden on Nw ȝeres morn.
Þe Knyȝt of þe Grene Chapel men knowen me mony;
455 Forþi me for to fynde if þou fraysteȝ, fayleȝ þou neuer.
Þerfore com, oþer recreaunt be calde þe behoues."
With a runisch rout þe rayneȝ he torneȝ,
Halled out at þe hal dor, his hed in his hande,
Þat þe fyr of þe flynt flaȝe fro fole houes.

And roughly he reached out   where riders stood,
Latched on to his lovely head,   and lifted it up soon;
And then bounded to his bronc,   the bridle he catches,
435   Steps into the stirrups,   strides aloft,
And his head by the hair   holds in his hand,
And as steadily the stalwart   sat him in his saddle,
As if no mishap had ailed him,   though headless now
       Instead.
440   He twisted his trunk about,
   That ugly body that bled;
   Many feared the clout,
   Ere his speech was said,

For the head in his hand   he holds upright,
445   Toward the dearest on the dais   he addresses the face,
And it lifted up the eye-lids   and looked full widely about
And spoke thus much with its mouth,   as you may now hear:
"Look, Gawain, thou be prepared   to go as thou promised,
And look loyally till thou,   liegeman, find me,
450   As thou hast promised in this hall,   in these knights' hearing;
To the Green Chapel choose the way,   I charge thee, to fetch
Such a dint as thou hast dealt   —thou hast deserved it—
To be promptly yielded   on New Year's morn.
As the Knight of the Green Chapel,   men know me many.
455   Thus me for to find, if thou set forth,   failest thou never.
Therefore come or recreant   to be called thee deservest."
With a rough roar   the reins he turns,
Hurried out at the hall door,   his head in his hand,
That the fire of the flint flew   from his foal's hooves.

460   To quat kyth he becom knwe non þere,

Neuer more þen þay wyste from queþen he watȝ wonnen.

       What þenne?

    Þe kyng and Gawen þare

    At þat grene þay laȝe and grenne,

465   Ȝet breued watȝ hit ful bare

    A meruayl among þo menne.

Þaȝ Arþer, þe hende kyng, at hert hade wonder,

He let no semblaunt be sene, bot sayde ful hyȝe

To þe comlych quene wyth cortays speche,

470   "Dere dame, to-day demay yow neuer;

Wel bycommes such craft vpon Cristmasse,

Laykyng of enterludeȝ, to laȝe and to syng,

Among þise kynde caroles of knyȝteȝ and ladyeȝ.

Neuer þe lece to my mete I may me wel dres,

475   For I haf sen a selly, I may not forsake."

He glent vpon Sir Gawen and gaynly he sayde,

"Now, sir, heng vp þyn ax, þat hatȝ innoȝ hewen";

And hit watȝ don abof þe dece on doser to henge,

Þer alle men for meruayl myȝt on hit loke,

480   And bi trwe tytel þerof to telle þe wonder.

Þenne þay boȝed to a borde þise burnes togeder,

Þe kyng and þe gode knyȝt, and kene men hem serued

Of alle dayntyeȝ double, as derrest myȝt falle;

Wyth alle maner of mete and mynstralcie boþe,

460   To what country that he came   knew none there,

        No more than they knew   from whence he was come.

              What then?

           The king and Gawain there

           At that green one they laugh and grin,

465   Yet recorded it was with care

           As a marvel among those men.

        Though Arthur, the elegant king,   at heart had wonder,

        He let no sign be seen,   but said full high

        To the comely queen   with courteous speech,

470   "Dear dame, today   dismay you never;

        Well becomes such craft   upon Christmas,

        Playing of interludes   to laugh and to sing,

        Among these courtly carols   of knights and ladies.

        Nonetheless to my meal   I may me well address,

475   For I have seen a strange sight;   I can not gainsay it."

        He glanced at Sir Gawain   and goodly he said,

        "Now sir, hang up thine ax,   that has enough hewed";

        And it was done, above the dais   on the tapestry hanging,

        Where all men for a marvel   might look on it

480   And be truly entitled there-of   to tell the wonder.

        Then they bounded to the board,   these battlers together,

        The king and the good knight,   and keen men them served

        With all dainties double,   as to the dearest should befall;

        With all manner of meat   and minstrelsy both,

485 Wyth wele walt þe day, til worþed an ende
in londe.
Now þenk wel, Sir Gawan,
For woþe þat þou ne wonde
Þis auenture for to frayn
490 Þat þou hatȝ tan on honde.

485   With wealth dwelt they that day,   until it went to an end
                In land.
               Now, think well, Sir Gawain,
               Lest for fear of what thou began,
               Thou from this adventure refrain
490   That thou hast taken in hand.

II

This hanselle hatʒ Arthur of auenturus on fyrst
In ʒonge ʒer, for he ʒerned ʒelpyng to here.
Thaʒ hym wordeʒ were wane when þay to sete wenten,
Now ar þay stoken of sturne werk, stafful her hond.

495   Gawan watʒ glad to begynne þose gomneʒ in halle,
Bot þaʒ þe ende be heuy haf ʒe no wonder;
For þaʒ men ben mery in mynde quen þay han mayn drynk,
A ʒere ʒernes ful ʒerne, and ʒeldeʒ neuer lyke;
Þe forme to þe fynisment foldeʒ ful selden.

500   Forþi þis ʒol ouerʒede, and þe ʒere after,
And vche sesoun serlepes sued after oþer:
After Crystenmasse com þe crabbed lentoun,
Þat fraysteʒ flesch wyth þe fysche and fode more symple;
Bot þenne þe weder of þe worlde wyth wynter hit þrepeʒ;

505   Colde clengeʒ adoun, cloudeʒ vplyften,
Schyre schedeʒ þe rayn in schowreʒ ful warme,
Falleʒ vpon fayre flat, flowreʒ þere schewen.
Boþe groundeʒ and þe greueʒ grene ar her wedeʒ;
Bryddeʒ busken to bylde, and bremlych syngen

510   For solace of þe softe somer þat sues þerafter
                bi bonk;
            And blossumeʒ bolne to blowe
            Bi raweʒ rych and ronk,
            Þen noteʒ noble innoʒe

515   Ar herde in wod so wlonk.

After þe sesoun of somer wyth þe soft wyndeʒ
Quen ʒeferus syfleʒ hymself on sedeʒ and erbeʒ,
Wela wynne is þe wort þat waxes þeroute,
When þe donkande dewe dropeʒ of þe leueʒ,

This gift has Arthur   of adventures at first
In the young year,   for he yearned to hear challenges.
Though words were wanting   when they went to sit,
Now are they stocked with stern work,   stuffed full their hands.
495   Gawain was glad to begin   those games in hall,
But though the end be heavy,   have ye no wonder;
For though men are merry   when they drink much,
A year runs full swiftly,   and yields never the same;
The first part with the finish   fits full seldom.
500   Thus this Yule passed by,   and the year after,
And each season separately   ensued after other:
After Christmas came   the crabbed Lent,
That tests the flesh with fish   and food more simple;
But then the weather of the world   wrangles with winter;
505   Cold clings down,   clouds uplift,
Shining sheds the rain   in showers full warm,
Falls upon fair fields;   flowers there show.
In both ground and the groves   green are their weeds;
Birds bustle to build,   and beautifully sing
510   For solace of the soft summer   that ensues there-after
            With thanks;
        And blossoms begin to swell
        By hedge-rows rich and rank,
        Then noble notes in the dell
515   Are heard in brush and banks.

After the season of summer   with the soft winds
When Zephyrus settles himself   on seeds and herbs,
Very well is the worthy plant   that waxes there-about,
When the drenching dew   drops from the leaves,

520   To bide a blysful blusch of þe bryȝt sunne.

       Bot þen hyȝes Heruest, and hardenes hym sone,

       Warneȝ hym for þe wynter to wax ful rype;

       He dryues wyth droȝt þe dust for to ryse,

       Fro þe face of þe folde to flyȝe ful hyȝe;

525   Wroþe wynde of þe welkyn wrasteleȝ with þe sunne,

       Þe leueȝ lancen fro þe lynde and lyȝten on þe grounde,

       And al grayes þe gres þat grene watȝ ere;

       Þenne al rypeȝ and roteȝ þat ros vpon fyrst,

       And þus ȝerneȝ þe ȝere in ȝisterdayeȝ mony,

530   And wynter wyndeȝ aȝayn, as þe worlde askeȝ,

              no fage,

        Til Meȝelmas mone

        Watȝ cumen wyth wynter wage;

        Þen þenkke Gawan ful sone

535   Of his anious uyage.

       Ȝet quyl Al-Hal-Day with Arþer he lenges;

       And he made a fare on þat fest for þe frekeȝ sake,

       With much reuel and ryche of þe Rounde Table.

       Knyȝteȝ ful cortays and comlych ladies

540   Al for luf of þat lede in longynge þay were,

       Bot neuer þe lece ne þe later þay neuened bot merþe.

       Mony ioyleȝ for þat ientyle iapeȝ þer maden.

       For after mete with mournyng he meleȝ to his eme,

       And spekeȝ of his passage, and pertly he sayde,

545   "Now, lege lorde of my lyf, leue I yow ask;

       Ȝe knowe þe cost of þis cace, kepe I no more;

       To telle yow teneȝ þerof neuer bot trifel;

       Bot I am boun to þe bur barely to-morne

       To sech þe gome of þe grene, as God wyl me wysse."

520 To abide a blissful blush   of the bright sun.
But then hurries in Harvest,   and hardens him soon,
Warns him for the winter   to wax full ripe;
He drives with drought   the dust for to rise,
From the face of the field   to fly full high;
525 Wrathful wind of the heavens   wrestles with the sun,
The leaves launch from the limbs   and alight on the ground,
And all grays the grass   that green was before;
Then all ripens and rots   that arose at first,
And thus yields the year   in yesterdays many,
530 And winter winds back again,   as the world asks
       For its age,
    Until Michaelmas moon
    Was come with winter's wage;
    Then thinks Gawain full soon
535   Of his anxious voyage.

Yet until All Saints' Day   with Arthur he lingers;
And he made a festival and a feast   for the fighter's sake,
With much revel and richness   of the Round Table.
Knights full courteous   and comely ladies
540 All for love of that lad   in longing they were,
But never the less nor the latter   they spoke only of mirth.
Many joyless for that gentle one   jests there made.
At after-meal with mourning   he communes with his uncle,
And speaks of his passage,   and plainly he said,
545 "Now, liege lord of my life,   leave I ask you;
Ye know the cost of this case,   care I no more;
To tell you troubles there-of   is nothing but trifle;
But I am bound to go   for the blow on tomorrow
To seek the gallant of the green,   as God will me guide."

43

550 Þenne þe best of þe burȝ boȝed togeder,
     Aywan, and Errik, and oþer ful mony,
     Sir Doddinaual de Sauage, þe duk of Clarence,
     Launcelot, and Lyonel, and Lucan þe gode,
     Sir Boos, and Sir Byduer, big men boþe,
555 And mony oþer menskful, with Mador de la Port.
     Alle þis compayny of court com þe kyng nerre
     For to counseyl þe knyȝt, with care at her hert.
     Þere watȝ much derue doel driuen in þe sale
     Þat so worthé as Wawan schulde wende on þat ernde,
560 To dryȝe a delful dynt, and dele no more
               wyth bronde.
          Þe knyȝt mad ay god chere,
          And sayde, "Quat schuld I wonde?
          Of destinés derf and dere
565   What may mon do bot fonde?"

     He dowelleȝ þer al þat day, and dresseȝ on þe morn,
     Askeȝ erly hys armeȝ, and alle were þay broȝt.
     Fyrst a tulé tapit tyȝt ouer þe flet,
     And miche watȝ þe gyld gere þat glent þeralofte;
570 Þe stif mon steppeȝ þeron, and þe stel hondeleȝ,
     Dubbed in a dublet of a dere tars,
     And syþen a crafty capados, closed aloft,
     Þat wyth a bryȝt blaunner was bounden withinne.
     Þenne set þay þe sabatounȝ vpon þe segge foteȝ,
575 His legeȝ lapped in stel with luflych greueȝ,
     With polayneȝ piched þerto, policed ful clene,
     Aboute his kneȝ knaged wyth knoteȝ of golde;
     Queme quyssewes þen, þat coyntlych closed
     His thik þrawen þyȝeȝ with þwonges to tachched;

44

550 Then the best of the burg   banded together:
Ywain and Eric,   and others full many,
Sir Dodinal de Savage,   the duke of Clarence,
Launcelot and Lionel,   and Lucan the good,
Sir Bors and Sir Bedivere,   big men both,
555 And many other men of worth,   with Mador de la Port.
All the company of court   came to the king nearer
For to counsel the knight,   with care at their hearts.
There was much secret sadness   suffered in the hall
That one so worthy as Wawain   should wend on that errand,
560 To endure a doleful dint,   and deal blows no more
        But die.
        The knight made ever good cheer,
        And said, "Why should I fly?
        Of destinies dreary or dear
565   What can man do but try?"

He dwells there all that day,   and dresses on the morn,
Asks early his arms,   and they were all brought.
First a red silk tapestry   spread tight on the floor,
And much was the gilded gear   that gleamed there-on;
570 The stout man steps upon it,   and the steel handles,
Adorned in a doublet   of a dear Turkish silk,
And next a clever leather cape,   closed at the throat,
That with bright white ermine   was bound within.
Then set they the steel shoes   upon the stalwart's feet,
575 His legs lapped in steel   with lovely armor,
With knee-plates placed there-to,   polished full bright,
About his knees knitted   with knots of gold;
Clear plate then,   that cleverly enclosed
His thick sinewed thighs,   with thongs attached;

45

580   And syþen þe brawden bryné of bryȝt stel ryngeȝ

    Vmbeweued þat wyȝ vpon wlonk stuffe,

    And wel bornyst brace vpon his boþe armes,

    With gode cowters and gay, and gloueȝ of plate,

    And alle þe godlych gere þat hym gayn schulde

585   þat tyde;

        Wyth ryche cote-armure,

        His gold spore spend with pryde,

        Gurde wyth a bront ful sure

        With silk sayn vmbe his syde.

590   When he watȝ hasped in armes, his harnays watȝ ryche:

    Þe lest lachet ouer loupe lemed of golde.

    So harnayst as he watȝ he herkneȝ his masse,

    Offred and honoured at þe heȝe auter.

    Syþen he comeȝ to þe kyng and to his cort-fereȝ,

595   Lacheȝ lufly his leue at lordeȝ and ladyeȝ;

    And þay hym kyst and conueyed, bikende hym to Kryst.

    Bi þat watȝ Gryngolet grayth, and gurde with a sadel

    Þat glemed ful gayly with mony golde frenges,

    Ayquere naylet ful nwe, for þat note ryched;

600   Þe brydel barred aboute, with bryȝt golde bounden;

    Þe apparayl of þe payttrure and of þe proude skyrteȝ,

    Þe cropore and þe couertor, acorded wyth þe arsouneȝ;

    And al watȝ rayled on red ryche golde nayleȝ,

    Þat al glytered and glent as glem of þe sunne.

605   Þenne hentes he þe helme, and hastily hit kysses,

    Þat watȝ stapled stifly, and stoffed wythinne.

    Hit watȝ hyȝe on his hede, hasped bihynde,

    Wyth a lyȝtly vrysoun ouer þe auentayle,

    Enbrawden and bounden wyth þe best gemmeȝ

580 And next the braided mail shirt   of bright steel rings
     Enclosed that warrior   and his costly clothes,
     And well burnished bracers   on both his arms,
     With good elbow-guards and gay,   and gloves of steel,
     And all the goodly gear   that should be gainful to him,
585   At that tide;
        With rich coat of arms
        His gold spurs affixed with pride,
        Girt with a sword full sure,
        With silken sash round his side.

590 When he was clasped in armor,   his harness was rich:
     The least lacing or loop   gleamed of gold.
     So, harnessed as he was,   he hears his mass,
     Offered and honored   at the high altar.
     Then he comes to the king   and to his court-fellows,
595 Takes lovingly his leave   from lords and ladies;
     And they kissed and departed,   entrusting him to Christ.
     By then was Gringolet ready,   and girt with a saddle
     That gleamed full gaily   with many gold fringes,
     Everywhere riveted full new,   ready for that work;
600 The bridle with bars about,   with bright gold bound;
     The apparel of the trappings   and of its proud skirts,
     The crupper and the covering   accord with the saddle-bows;
     And all was arrayed   on rich red gold studs,
     That all glittered and glowed   as gleam of the sun.
605 Then takes he the helmet,   and hastily it kisses,
     That was stapled securely,   and stuffed with padding.
     It was high on his head,   held by a hasp behind,
     With a light silk band   over the neck piece,
     Embroidered and bedecked   with the best gems

610　On brode sylkyn borde, and bryddeʒ on semeʒ,
　　　As papiayeʒ paynted peruyng bitwene,
　　　Tortors and trulofeʒ entayled so þyk
　　　As mony burde þeraboute had ben seuen wynter
　　　　　　in toune.
615　　　Þe cercle watʒ more o prys
　　　　Þat vmbeclypped hys croun,
　　　　Of diamaunteʒ a deuys
　　　　Þat boþe were bryʒt and broun.

　　　Then þay schewed hym þe schelde, þat was of schyr gouleʒ
620　Wyth þe pentangel depaynt of pure golde hweʒ.
　　　He braydeʒ hit by þe bauderyk, aboute þe hals kestes;
　　　Þat bisemed þe segge semlyly fayre.
　　　And quy þe pentangel apendeʒ to þat prynce noble
　　　I am in tent yow to telle, þof tary hyt me schulde:
625　Hit is a syngne þat Salamon set sumquyle
　　　In bytoknyng of trawþe, bi tytle þat hit habbeʒ,
　　　For hit is a figure þat haldeʒ fyue poynteʒ,
　　　And vche lyne vmbelappeʒ and loukeʒ in oþer,
　　　And ayquere hit is endeleʒ; and Englych hit callen
630　Oueral, as I here, þe endeles knot.
　　　Forþy hit acordeʒ to þis knyʒt and to his cler armeʒ,
　　　For ay faythful in fyue and sere fyue syþeʒ:
　　　Gawan watʒ for gode knawen, and as golde pured,
　　　Voyded of vche vylany, wyth vertueʒ ennourned
635　　　　　in mote;
　　　　Forþy þe pentangel nwe
　　　　He ber in schelde and cote,
　　　　As tulk of tale most trwe
　　　　And gentylest knyʒt of lote.

610　On broad silken borders,　and birds on the seams,
　　　Such as parrots painted　preening there-about,
　　　Turtle-doves and true-love knots　portrayed so thick
　　　As if many maids there-upon　had worked seven winters
　　　　　　　　　In town.
615　　　　　　　The circlet was worth more,
　　　　　　　That enclasped his crown,
　　　　　　　For diamonds by the score
　　　　　　　Shone brightly all around.

　　　Then they showed him the shield,　that was of shining red
620　With the pentangle depicted　in pure gold hues.
　　　He seizes it by the baldric,　about the neck casts;
　　　That well suits the stalwart　so seemly fair.
　　　And why the pentangle pertains　to that noble prince
　　　I intend you to tell,　though tarry me it should:
625　It is a sign that Solomon　set some time ago
　　　In betokening of troth,　that it truly has,
　　　For it is a figure　that holds five points,
　　　And each line embraces　and locks in the other,
　　　And everywhere it is endless;　and the English call it
630　All over, as I hear,　the endless knot.
　　　Therefore it accords to this knight　and to his bright arms,
　　　For ever faithful in five ways　and five times in each way:
　　　Gawain was for good known,　and as gold purified,
　　　Devoid of each villainy,　with virtues endowed
635　　　　　　　And devoted;
　　　　　　　Therefore the pentangle new
　　　　　　　He bore on shield and coat,
　　　　　　　As man of tale most true
　　　　　　　And gentlest knight of note.

640	Fyrst he watȝ funden fautleȝ in his fyue wytteȝ,
	And efte fayled neuer þe freke in his fyue fyngres,
	And alle his afyaunce vpon folde watȝ in þe fyue woundeȝ
	Þat Cryst kaȝt on þe croys, as þe Crede telleȝ;
	And quere-so-euer þys mon in melly watȝ stad,
645	His þro þoȝt watȝ in þat, þurȝ alle oþer þyngeȝ,
	Þat alle his forsnes he feng at þe Fyue Joyeȝ
	Þat þe hende heuen-quene had of hir chylde;
	At þis cause þe knyȝt comlyche hade
	In þe inore half of his schelde hir ymage depaynted,
650	Þat quen he blusched þerto his belde neuer payred.
	Þe fyft fyue þat I finde þat þe frek vsed
	Watȝ fraunchyse and felaȝschyp forbe al þyng,
	His clannes and his cortaysye croked were neuer,
	And pité, þat passeȝ alle poynteȝ, þyse pure fyue
655	Were harder happed on þat haþel þen on any oþer.
	Now alle þese fyue syþeȝ, for soþe, were fetled on þis knyȝt,
	And vchone halched in oþer, þat non ende hade,
	And fyched vpon fyue poynteȝ, þat fayld neuer,
	Ne samned neuer in no syde, ne sundred nouþer,
660	Withouten ende at any noke I oquere fynde,
	Whereeuer þe gomen bygan, or glod to an ende.
	Þerfore on his schene schelde schapen watȝ þe knot
	Ryally wyth red golde vpon rede gowleȝ,
	Þat is þe pure pentaungel wyth þe peple called
665	with lore.
	Now grayþed is Gawan gay,
	And laȝt his launce ryȝt þore,
	And gef hem alle goud day—
	He wende for euermore.

640   First he was found faultless   in his five wits,
       And also failed never the fighter   in his five fingers,
       And all his faith in the field   was in the five wounds
       That Christ caught on the cross,   as the Creed tells;
       And where-so-ever this man   in melee took a stand,
645   His steadfast thought was in that,   over all other things,
       That all his courage he took   from the Five Joys
       That the courteous heaven-queen   had of her child;
       For this cause   the comely knight had
       On the inside of his shield   her image depicted,
650   That when he looked there-to   he never lacked boldness.
       The fifth five that I find   that the fighter used
       Was generosity and fellowship   before all things,
       His purity and his courtesy   crooked were never,
       And pity, that passes all points;   these pure five
655   Were more heartily heaped   on that horseman than any other.
       Now all these five fives, forsooth,   were fixed on this knight,
       And each one woven into other,   so that no end it had,
       And fixed upon five points,   that failed never,
       Not assembled ever on one side,   nor separated neither,
660   Without end at any angle   anywhere, I find,
       Wherever the game began,   or had gone to an end.
       Therefore on his shining shield   shaped was the knot
       Royally with bright gold   upon a red background,
       That is the pure pentangle   by the people called
665   With lore.
          Now gracefully Gawain gay
          Latched on to his lance for war,
          And gave them all good day—
          He thought for evermore.

670 He sperred þe sted with þe spureȝ and sprong on his way,

So stif þat þe ston-fyr stroke out þerafter.

Al þat seȝ þat semly syked in hert,

And sayde soþly al same segges til oþer,

Carande for þat comly: "Bi Kryst, hit is scaþe

675 Þat þou, leude, schal be lost, þat art of lyf noble!

To fynde hys fere vpon folde, in fayth, is not eþe.

Warloker to haf wroȝt had more wyt bene,

And haf dyȝt ȝonder dere a duk to haue worþed;

A lowande leder of ledeȝ in londe hym wel semeȝ,

680 And so had better haf ben þen britned to noȝt,

Hadet wyth an aluisch mon, for angardeȝ pryde.

Who knew euer any kyng such counsel to take

As knyȝtes in cauelaciounȝ on Crystmasse gomneȝ?"

Wel much watȝ þe warme water þat waltered of yȝen,

685 When þat semly syre soȝt fro þo woneȝ

    þad daye.

        He made non abode,

        Bot wyȝtly went hys way;

        Mony wylsum way he rode,

690   Þe bok as I herde say.

Now rideȝ þis renk þurȝ þe ryalme of Logres,

Sir Gauan, on Godeȝ halue, þaȝ hym no gomen þoȝt.

Oft leudleȝ alone he lengeȝ on nyȝteȝ

Þer he fonde noȝt hym byfore þe fare þat he lyked.

695 Hade he no fere bot his fole bi frytheȝ and douneȝ,

Ne no gome bot God bi gate wyth to karp,

Til þat he neȝed ful neȝe into þe Norþe Waleȝ.

Alle þe iles of Anglesay on lyft half he haldeȝ,

670 He spurred the steed with the spurs   and sprang on his way,
So strong that the stone-fire   struck out there-after.
All that saw that seemly   sighed in heart,
And soothly all the same   said stalwarts to each other,
Caring for that comely: "By Christ, it is a calamity
675 That thou, liegeman, shall be lost,   that art of life noble!
To find his fellow upon field,   in faith, is not easy.
More warily to have worked   had been more wise,
And to have designated yonder dear   a duke to have become;
An illustrious leader of lads   in land could well be,
680 And had better have been that   than battered to nothing,
Beheaded by a monstrous man,   for arrogant pride.
Who knew ever any king   such counsel to take
As from knights quibbling   about Christmas games?"
Well much was the warm water   that weltered from eyes,
685 When that seemly sire   set out from those dwellings
    That day.
    He turned to the road,
    And stoutly went his way;
    Many bewildering routes he rode,
690   The book as I heard say.

Now rides this rider   through the realm of Logres,
Sir Gawain, by God's wounds,   though no game it seemed.
Oft friendless alone   he lingers by night
Where he found not before him   the fare that he liked.
695 Had he no friend but his foal   by forests and downs,
Nor no gallant but God   to speak with by the way,
Till that he nighed full nigh   into the North Wales.
All the isles of Anglesey   on left side he holds,

And fareʒ ouer þe fordeʒ by þe forlondeʒ,
700 Ouer at þe Holy Hede, til he hade eft bonk
In þe wyldrenesse of Wyrale; wonde þer bot lyte
Þat auþer God oþer gome wyth goud hert louied.
And ay he frayned, as he ferde, at frekeʒ þat he met,
If þay hade herde any karp of a knyʒt grene,
705 In any grounde þeraboute, of þe Grene Chapel;
And al nykked hym wyth "nay," þat neuer in her lyue
Þay seʒe neuer no segge þat watʒ of suche hweʒ
    of grene.
        Þe knyʒt tok gates straunge
710   In mony a bonk vnbene;
        His cher ful oft con chaunge
        Þat chapel er he myʒt sene.

Mony klyf he ouerclambe in contrayeʒ straunge,
Fer floten fro his frendeʒ fremedly he rydeʒ.
715 At vche warþe oþer water þer þe wʒye passed
He fonde a foo hym byfore—bot ferly hit were—
And þat so foule and so felle þat feʒt hym byhode.
So mony meruayl bi mount þer þe mon fyndeʒ,
Hit were to tore for to telle of þe tenþe dole.
720 Sumwhyle wyth wormeʒ he werreʒ, and with wolues als,
Sumwhyle wyth wodwos, þat woned in þe knarreʒ,
Boþe wyth bulleʒ and bereʒ, and boreʒ oþerquyle,
And etayneʒ, þat hym anelede of þe heʒe felle;
Nade he ben duʒty and dryʒe, and Dryʒtyn had serued,
725 Douteles he hade ben ded and dreped ful ofte.
For werre wrathed hym not so much þat wynter nas wors,
When þe colde cler water fro þe cloudeʒ schadde,
And fres er hit falle myʒt to þe fale erþe;

54

And fares over the fords   by the forelands,
700   Over by the Holyhead,   until he again had the shore
In the wilderness of Wirral;   dwelt there but few
That neither God nor man   with good heart loved.
And ever he asked, as he fared,   from folk that he met,
If they had heard any talk   of a green knight,
705   On any ground there-about,   or of a Green Chapel;
And all denied it with "nay,"   that never in their lives
They ever saw any stalwart   that was of such hues
      Of green.
     The knight took ways strange
710   In many a bank between;
     His mood full oft did change
     Ere that chapel might be seen.

Many a cliff he overclimbed   in countries strange,
Far flown from his friends   as a foreigner he rides.
715   At each shore or water   where the warrior passed
He found a foe before him—   else a wonder it was—
And that so foul and so fierce   that to fight him behooved.
So many marvels by mountains   there the man finds,
It were too toilsome for to tell   of the tenth part.
720   Sometimes with dragons he wars,   and with wolves also,
Sometimes with wild men,   that dwelt in the woods,
Both with bulls and bears,   and boars at other times,
And ogres, that him annoyed   from the high rocks;
Were he not doughty and enduring,   and the dear Lord served,
725   Doubtless he had been dead   and done for full oft.
For war worried him not so much;   that winter was worse,
When the cold clear water   from the clouds shed,
And froze ere it fall might   to the faded earth;

Ner slayn wyth þe slete he sleped in his yrnes

730   Mo nyȝteȝ þen innoȝe in naked rokkeȝ,

Þer as claterande fro þe crest þe colde borne renneȝ,

And henged hege ouer his hede in hard iisse-ikkles.

Þus in peryl and payne and plytes ful harde

Bi contray cayreȝ þis knyȝt, tyl Krystmasse euen,

735   al one;

       Þe knyȝt wel þat tyde

       To Mary made his mone,

       Þat ho hym red to ryde

       And wysse hym to sum wone.

740   Bi a mounte on þe morne meryly he rydes

Into a forest ful dep, þat ferly watȝ wylde,

Hiȝe hilleȝ on vche a halue, and holtwodeȝ vnder

Of hore okeȝ ful hoge a hundreth togeder;

Þe hasel and þe haȝþorne were harled al samen,

745   With roȝe raged mosse rayled aywhere,

With mony bryddeȝ vnblyþe vpon bare twyges,

Þat pitosly þer piped for pyne of þe colde.

Þe gome vpon Gryngolet glydeȝ hem vnder,

Þurȝ mony misy and myre, mon al hym one,

750   Carande for his costes, lest he ne keuer schulde

To se þe seruyse of þat Syre, þat on þat self nyȝt

Of a burde watȝ borne oure baret to quelle;

And þerfore sykyng he sayde, "I beseche þe, Lorde,

And Mary, þat is myldest moder so dere,

755   Of sum herber þer heȝly I myȝt here masse,

Ande þy matyneȝ tomorne, mekely I ask,

Nearly slain with the sleet   he slept in his iron armor
730   More nights than enough   in naked rocks,
Where clattering from the crest   the cold brook runs,
And hanged high over his head   in hard icicles.
Thus in peril and pain   and plights full hard
Through the country comes this knight,   til Christmas eve,
735   Alone;
          The knight well that tide
          To Mary made his moan,
          That she reveal where to ride
          That some dwelling him be shown.

740   By a mount on the morn   merrily he rides
Into a forest full deep,   that was fabulously wild,
Tall hills on each side,   and high woods as well
Of hoar oaks full huge,   a hundred in all;
The hazel and the hawthorn   were tangled all together,
745   With rough ragged moss   arrayed everywhere,
With many birds unblithe   upon bare twigs,
That piteously there piped   for pain of the cold.
The gallant upon Gringolet   galloped them under,
Through many a morass and mire,   a man all alone,
750   Caring for his duties,   lest he should not come
To see the service of that Sire   that on that same night
Of a maiden was born   our troubles to abate;
And there-for sighing he said,   "I beseech thee, Lord,
And Mary, that is mildest   mother so dear,
755   For some harborage where holily   I might hear mass,
And thy matins in the morning,   meekly I ask,

And þerto prestly I pray my Pater and Aue
    and Crede."
    He rode in his prayere,
760   And cryed for his mysdede;
    He sayned hym in syþes sere,
    And sayde "Cros Kryst me spede!"

Nade he sayned hymself, segge, bot þrye,
Er he watʒ war in þe wod of a won in a mote,
765 Abof a launde, on a lawe, loken vnder boʒeʒ
Of mony borelych bole aboute bi þe diches:
A castel þe comlokest þat euer knyʒt aʒte,
Pyched on a prayere, a park al aboute,
With a pyked palays pyned ful þik,
770 Þat vmbeteʒe mony tre mo þen two myle.
Þat holde on þat on syde þe haþel auysed,
As hit schemered and schon þurʒ þe schyre okeʒ;
Þenne hatʒ he hendly of his helme, and heʒly he þonkeʒ
Jesus and Sayn Gilyan, þat gentyle ar boþe,
775 Þat cortaysly had hym kydde, and his cry herkened.
"Now bone hostel," coþe þe burne, "I beseche yow ʒette!"
Þenne gerdeʒ he to Gryngolet with þe gilt heleʒ,
And he ful chauncely hatʒ chosen to þe chef gate,
Þat broʒt bremly þe burne to þe bryge ende
780   in haste.
    Þe bryge watʒ breme vpbrayde,
    Þe ʒateʒ wer stoken faste.
    Þe walleʒ were wel arayed,
    Hit dut no wyndeʒ blaste.

And there-to promptly I pray   my 'Our Father' and 'Hail Mary'
        And 'Creed.'"
    He rode in his prayer,
760   And cried for his misdeed;
    He signed himself repeatedly there,
    And said "Cross of Christ me lead!"

He had not signed himself,   that stalwart, but thrice,
Ere he was aware in the wood   of a dwelling within a moat,
765 Above an open lawn, on a low hill,   locked under boughs
By many burly branches   about by the ditches:
A castle the comeliest   that ever knight commanded,
Placed on an open meadow,   a park all around,
With a spiked palisade   penned in full thick,
770 That enclosed many trees   more than two miles.
That hold on that one side   the horseman observed,
As it shimmered and shone   through sheltering oaks;
Then courteously he doffs his helmet,   and holily he thanks
Jesus and Saint Julian,   that gentle are both,
775 Who courteously recognized him,   and his cry hearkened.
    "Now for good lodging," quoth the brave,   "I beseech you yet!"
Then he gives spur to Gringolet   with the gilded heels,
And he fully by chance has chosen   the chief path,
That quickly brought the brave   to the bridge's end
780   In haste.
        The bridge was firmly raised,
        The gates were shut up fast.
        The walls were mightily made;
        They feared no windy blast.

785　　　Þe burne bode on blonk, þat on bonk houed
　　　　　Of þe depe double dich þat drof to þe place;
　　　　　Þe walle wod in þe water wonderly depe,
　　　　　Ande eft a ful huge he3t hit haled vpon lofte
　　　　　Of harde hewen ston vp to þe table3,
790　　　Enbaned vnder þe abataylment in þe best lawe;
　　　　　And syþen garyte3 ful gaye gered bitwene,
　　　　　Wyth mony luflych loupe þat louked ful clene;
　　　　　A better barbican þat burne blusched vpon neuer.
　　　　　And innermore he behelde þat halle ful hy3e,
795　　　Towres telded bytwene, trochet ful þik,
　　　　　Fayre fylyole3 þat fy3ed, and ferlyly long,
　　　　　With coruon coprounes craftyly sle3e.
　　　　　Chalkwhyt chymnees þer ches he inno3e
　　　　　Vpon bastel roue3, þat blenked ful quyte.
800　　　So mony pynakle payntet wat3 poudred ayquere,
　　　　　Among þe castel carnele3 clambred so þik,
　　　　　Þat pared out of papure purely hit semed.
　　　　　Þe fre freke on þe fole hit fayr inno3e þo3t,
　　　　　If he my3t keuer to com þe cloyster wythinne,
805　　　To herber in þat hostel whyl halyday lested,
　　　　　　　　　auinant.
　　　　　　　　He calde, and sone þer com
　　　　　　　　A porter pure plesaunt,
　　　　　　　　On þe wal his ernd he nome
810　　　　　And haylsed þe kny3t erraunt.

　　　　　"Gode sir," quoþ Gawan, "wolde3 þou go myn ernde
　　　　　To þe he3 lorde of þis hous, herber to craue?"
　　　　　"3e, Peter," quoþ þe porter, "and purely I trowee

785 The brave abided on his bronc, that hovered on the bank
   Of the deep double ditch that defended the place;
   The wall went into the water wonderfully deep,
   And then a full huge height it had upon loft
   Of hard hewed stone high up to the cornices
790 With ledges under the battlements in the best style;
   And then towers full gay placed goodly between
   With many lovely windows that locked completely;
   A better defense that brave looked upon never.
   And further in he beheld that hall full high,
795 Towers between them, pinnacles full thick,
   Fair spires that befitted them, and fabulously high,
   With curiously carved tops, craftily made.
   Chalk-white chimneys, many choice ones
   On the burg's roofs, that shone bright white.
800 So many painted pinnacles were put about everywhere,
   About the castle embrasures clustered so thick,
   That pared out of paper surely it seemed.
   The fighter on his foal thought it fair indeed,
   If he could have leave to come the cloister within,
805 To have harbor in that hostel while the holy days last,
      As at present.
     He called, and soon there came
     A porter purely pleasant,
     On the wall his duty to proclaim
810   And hail the knight errant.

  "Good sir," quoth Gawain, "wouldst thou go my errand
   To the high lord of this house, lodging to crave?"
   "Yea, Peter," quoth the porter, "and surely I suppose

Þat ȝe be, wyȝe, welcum to won quyle yow lykeȝ."

815 Þen ȝede þe wyȝe ȝerne and com aȝayn swyþe,
And folke frely hym wyth, to fonge þe knyȝt.
Þay let doun þe grete draȝt and derely out ȝeden,
And kneled doun on her knes vpon þe colde erþe
To welcum þis ilk wyȝ as worþy hom þoȝt;

820 Þay ȝolden hym þe brode ȝate, ȝarked vp wyde,
And he hem raysed rekenly, and rod ouer þe brygge.
Sere seggeȝ hym sesed by sadel, quel he lyȝt,
And syþen stabeled his stede stif men innoȝe.
Knyȝteȝ and swyereȝ comen doun þenne

825 For to bryng þis buurne wyth blys into halle;
Quen he hef vp his helme, þer hiȝed innoghe
For to hent hit at his honde, þe hende to seruen;
His bronde and his blasoun boþe þay token.
Þen haylsed he ful hendly þo haþeleȝ vchone,

830 And mony proud mon þer presed þat prynce to honour.
Alle hasped in his heȝ wede to halle þay hym wonnen,
Þer fayre fyre vpon flet fersly brenned.
Þenne þe lorde of þe lede louteȝ fro his chambre
For to mete wyth menske þe mon on þe flor;

835 He sayde, "Ȝe ar welcum to welde as yow lykeȝ
Þat here is; al is yowre awen, to haue at yowre wylle
      and welde."
         "Graunt mercy," quoþ Gawayn,
         "Þer Kryst hit yow forȝelde."

840 As frekeȝ þat semed fayn
   Ayþer oþer in armeȝ con felde.

Gawayn glyȝt on þe gome þat godly hym gret,
And þuȝt hit a bolde burne þat þe burȝ aȝte,

62

That ye be, warrior, welcome   to dwell while you like."
815   Then went the warrior eagerly   and came again quickly,
And folk courteously with him,   to accompany the knight.
They let down the great draw-bridge   and decorously went,
And kneeled down on their knees   upon the cold earth
To welcome this same warrior   as worthy they thought;
820   They yield to him the broad gate,   gaping up wide,
And he bad them rise readily,   and rode over the bridge.
Several stalwarts held his saddle,   while he stepped down,
And then stabled his steed   stout men many.
Knights and squires   came down then
825   For to bring this brave   with bliss into hall;
When he heaved up his helmet,   there hastened many
For to have it from his hand,   the courtier to honor;
His broad sword and his blazoned shield   both they took.
Then hailed he full courteously   those horsemen each one,
830   And many proud men there pressed in,   that prince to honor.
All harnessed in his high armor   to hall they bring him
Where fair fire upon floor   fiercely burned.
Then the lord of the lads   leaves his chamber
For to meet with good manners   the man on the floor;
835   He said, "Ye are welcome,   to wield what you like
All that is here is your own,   to have at your will
            And hold."
         "Great thanks," quoth Gawain,
         "May Christ you uphold."
840   As fighters that do not feign
         Each other in arms did enfold.

Gawain gazed on the gallant   that goodly him greeted,
And thought it a bold brave   that the burg owned,

A hoge haþel for þe noneȝ, and of hyghe eldee;

845 Brode, bryȝt, watȝ his berde, and al beuer-hwed,

Sturne, stif on þe stryþþe on stalworth schonkeȝ,

Felle face as þe fyre, and fre of hys speche;

And wel hym semed, for soþe, as þe segge þuȝt,

To lede a lortschyp in lee of leudeȝ ful gode.

850 Þe lorde hym charred to a chambre, and chefly cumaundeȝ

To delyuer hym a leude, hym loȝly to serue;

And þere were boun at his bode burneȝ innoȝe,

Þat broȝt hym to a bryȝt boure, þer beddyng watȝ noble,

Of cortynes of clene sylk wyth cler golde hemmeȝ,

855 And couertoreȝ ful curious with comlych paneȝ

Of bryȝt blaunner aboue, enbrawded bisydeȝ,

Rudeleȝ rennande on ropeȝ, red golde ryngeȝ,

Tapiteȝ tyȝt to þe woȝe of Tuly and Tars,

And vnder fete, on þe flet, of folȝande sute.

860 Þer he watȝ dispoyled, wyth specheȝ of myerþe,

Þe burn of his bruny and of his bryȝt wedeȝ.

Ryche robes ful rad renkkeȝ hym broȝten,

For to charge, and to chaunge, and chose of þe best.

Sone as he on hent, and happed þerinne,

865 Þat sete on hym semly wyth saylande skyrteȝ,

Þe ver by his uisage verayly hit semed

Welneȝ to vche haþel, alle on hwes

Lowande and lufly alle his lymmeȝ vnder,

Þat a comloker knyȝt neuer Kryst made

870   hem þoȝt.

        Wheþen in worlde he were,

        Hit semed as he moȝt

        Be prynce withouten pere

        In felde þer felle men foȝt.

64

A huge horseman for battling,   and in his best years;
845   Broad, bright, was his beard,   and all beaver-colored,
Stern, strong in his stance   on stalwart shanks,
Face fierce as the fire,   and fair in his speech;
And well him suited, for sooth,   as the stalwart thought,
To lead a lordship in a castle   of liegemen full good.
850   The lord conducts him to a chamber,   and quickly commands
To assign him a lad,   loyally to serve;
And there were ready at his bidding   many brave knights,
That brought him to a bright bower,   with noble bedding,
Of curtains of glowing silk   with gleaming gold hems,
855   And covers full curious   with comely panels
Of bright white fur above,   embroidered round about,
Curtains running on ropes,   with red gold rings,
Stretched on the wall tapestries   of Toulouse and Turkestan,
And under foot, on the floor,   of a matching form.
860   There he was disarmed,   with speeches of mirth,
The brave of his mail   and of his bright armor.
Rich robes full readily   servants him brought,
For to choose one, and to change,   and rejoice in the best.
As soon as he has picked one,   and is apparelled within
865   One that sat on him seemly   with spreading skirts,
The verdant Spring by his visage   verily it seemed
Well nigh to each horsemen,   for all its hues
Glowing and lovely,   and all his limbs covered,
That a comelier knight   never Christ made,
870   They thought.
          Wherever in world he were,
          It seemed as if he ought
          Be prince without peer
          In field where fierce men fought.

65

875	A cheyer byfore þe chemné, þer charcole brenned,
	Watʒ grayþed for Sir Gawan grayþely with cloþeʒ,
	Whyssynes vpon queldepoyntes þat koynt wer boþe;
	And þenne a meré mantyle watʒ on þat mon cast
	Of a broun bleeaunt, enbrauded ful ryche
880	And fayre furred wythinne with felleʒ of þe best,
	Alle of ermyn in erde, his hode of þe same;
	And he sete in þat settel semlych ryche,
	And achaufed hym chefly, and þenne his cher mended.
	Sone watʒ telded vp a tabil on tresteʒ ful fayre,
885	Clad wyth a clene cloþe þat cler quyt schewed,
	Sanap, and salure, and syluerin sponeʒ.
	Þe wyʒe wesche at his wylle, and went to his mete.
	Seggeʒ hym serued semly innoʒe
	Wyth sere sewes and sete, sesounde of þe best.
890	Double-felde, as hit falleʒ, and fele kyn fischeʒ,
	Summe baken in bred, summe brad on þe gledeʒ,
	Summe soþen, summe in sewe sauered with spyces,
	And ay sawes so sleye þat þe segge lyked.
	Þe freke calde hit a fest ful frely and ofte
895	Ful hendely, quen alle þe haþeles rehayted hym at oneʒ,
	as hende,
	"Þis penaunce now ʒe take,
	And eft hit schal amende."
	Þat mon much merþe con make,
900	For wyn in his hed þat wende.

	Þenne watʒ spyed and spured vpon spare wyse
	Bi preué poynteʒ of þat prynce, put to hymseluen,
	Þat he beknew cortaysly of þe court þat he were

875 A chair before the chimney, where charcoal burned,
   Was arrayed for Sir Gawain gracefully with cloths,
   Cushions upon quilts that were all cleverly made;
   And then a merry mantle was on that man cast
   Of a bright silk fabric, embroidered full rich
880 And fair furred within with the finest of pelts,
   All with ermine adorned, his hood of the same;
   And he sat in that seat, sumptuously rich,
   And warmed himself quickly, and then his mood changed.
   Soon was set up a table on trestles full fair,
885 Clad with a gleaming cloth that clear white shone,
   Place-mats, and saltcellars, and silver spoons.
   The warrior washed, as he wished, and went to his meal.
   Stalwarts him served seemly indeed
   With many excellent stews, seasoned of the best,
890 Double portions, as was fitting, and fish of many kinds,
   Some baked in bread, some broiled on the coals,
   Some seethed, some in stews savored with spices,
   And always subtle sauces that the stalwart liked.
   The fighter called it a feast full freely and oft
895 Full courteously, when all the horsemen a reply at once
      Extended:
     "This penance now ye take,
     And soon it shall be amended."
     That man much mirth did make,
900   For wine in his head that wended.

   Then was spied out and asked in subtle ways
   By privy questions of that prince, put to himself,
   That he admitted courteously that he was of the court

Þat aþel Arthure þe hende haldeʒ hym one,

905 Þat is þe ryche ryal kyng of þe Rounde Table,

And hit watʒ Wawen hymself þat in þat won sytteʒ,

Comen to þat Krystmasse, as case hym þen lymped.

When þe lorde hade lerned þat he þe leude hade,

Loude laʒed he þerat, so lef hit hym þoʒt,

910 And alle þe men in þat mote maden much joye

To apere in his presense prestly þat tyme,

Þat alle prys and prowes and pured þewes

Apendes to hys persoun, and praysed is euer;

Byfore alle men vpon molde his mensk is þe most.

915 Vch segge ful softly sayde to his fere:

"Now schal we semlych se sleʒteʒ of þeweʒ

And þe teccheles termes of talkyng noble,

Wich spede is in speche vnspurd may we lerne,

Syn we haf fonged þat fyne fader of nurture.

920 God hatʒ geuen vus his grace godly for soþe,

Þat such a gest as Gawan graunteʒ vus to haue,

When burneʒ blyþe of his burþe schal sitte

          and synge.

    In menyng of mandereʒ mere

925   Þis burne now schal vus bryng;

    I hope þat may hym here

    Schal lerne of luf-talkyng."

Bi þat þe diner watʒ done and þe dere vp

Hit watʒ neʒ at þe nyʒt neʒed þe tyme.

930 Chaplayneʒ to þe chapeles chosen þe gate,

Rungen ful rychely, ryʒt as þay schulden,

To þe hersum euensong of þe hyʒe tyde.

That Arthur the elegant   holds as his own,
905 He who is the rich royal king   of the Round Table,
And it was Gawain himself   that in that hall sits,
Come to that Christmas,   as the case then befell.
When the lord had learned   that he this liegeman had,
Loud laughed he there-at,   so lovely it seemed to him,
910 And all the men inside that moat   made much joy
To appear in his presence   promptly that time,
Since all price and prowess   and pure manners
Append to his person,   and praised are ever;
Before all men upon earth   his honor is the most.
915 Each stalwart full softly   said to his fellow:
"Now shall we surely see   the skills of good manners
And the faultless terms   of talking noble.
What success is in speech   without asking we can learn,
Since we have found here   that fine father of nurture.
920 God has given us his grace   goodly for sooth,
Who such a guest as Gawain   grants us to have,
When blithe braves   of his birth shall sit
           And sing.
      To understand good manners here
925   This brave now shall us bring;
      I hold that he who may him hear
      Shall learn of love-talking."

When dinner was done   and the dear Gawain up
It was nigh to that time   that night neared.
930 Chaplains to the chapels   chose the direct way,
Rang full richly,   right as they should,
To the holy Evensong   of the high season.

Þe lorde loutes þerto, and þe lady als;
Into a cumly closet coyntly ho entreȝ.
935 Gawan glydeȝ ful gay and gos þeder sone;
Þe lorde laches hym by þe lappe and ledeȝ hym to sytte,
And couþly hym knoweȝ and calleȝ hym his nome,
And sayde he watȝ þe welcomest wyȝe of þe worlde;
And he hym þonkked þroly, and ayþer halched oþer,
940 And seten soberly samen þe seruise quyle.
Þenne lyst þe lady to loke on þe knyȝt,
Þenne com ho of hir closet with mony cler burdeȝ.
Ho watȝ þe fayrest in felle, of flesche and of lyre,
And of compas and colour and costes, of alle oþer,
945 And wener þen Wenore, as þe wyȝe þoȝt.
He ches þurȝ þe chaunsel to cheryche þat hende.
An oþer lady hir lad bi þe lyft honde,
Þat watȝ alder þen ho, an auncian hit semed,
And heȝly honowred with haþeleȝ aboute.
950 Bot vnlyke on to loke þo ladyes were,
For if þe ȝonge watȝ ȝep, ȝolȝe watȝ þat oþer;
Riche red on þat on rayled ayquere,
Ruȝ ronkled chekeȝ þat oþer on rolled;
Kerchofes of þat on, wyth mony cler perleȝ,
955 Hir brest and hir bryȝt þrote bare displayed,
Schon schyrer þen snawe þat schedeȝ on hilleȝ;
Þat oþer wyth a gorger watȝ gered ouer þe swyre,
Chymbled ouer hir blake chyn with chalkquyte vayles,
Hir frount folden in sylk, enfoubled ayquere,
960 Toreted and treleted with tryfleȝ aboute,
Þat noȝt watȝ bare of þat burde bot þe blake broȝes,
Þe tweyne yȝen and þe nase, þe naked lyppeȝ,

The lord leads there-to,   and the lady also;
Into a comely enclosed pew   gracefully she enters.
935   Gawain goes full gay   and gets thither soon;
The lord snatches him by the sleeve   and leads him to sit,
And cordially with him converses   and calls him by his name,
And said he was the welcomest   warrior in the world;
And he him thanked thoroughly,   and either hugged the other,
940   And sat soberly together   during the service.
Then desired the lady   to look on the knight,
Then came she from her enclosed pew   with glowing maidens.
She was the fairest in complexion,   of flesh and of skin,
And of stature and color and customs,   compared to all others,
945   And more lovely than Guenevere,   as the warrior thought.
He chose his way through the sanctuary   to salute that lady.
Another lady her led   by the left hand,
That was older than she,   an ancient it seemed,
And highly honored   by horsemen about.
950   But unlike to look on   those ladies were,
For if the young was fresh,   yellowed was that other;
Rich red on that one   arrayed everywhere,
Rough wrinkled cheeks   rolled on that other;
Kerchiefs on that one,   with many clear pearls,
955   Her breast and her bright throat   bare displayed,
Shone more shining than snow   that sheds on hills;
That other with a collar   had covered all her neck,
Enclosed her black chin   with chalk-white veils,
Her forehead covered and adorned,   enfolded everywhere,
960   Bedecked and tricked out   bejeweled all round,
That nothing was bare of that woman   but the black brows,
The two eyes and the nose,   the naked lips,

71

And þose were soure to se and sellyly blered;
A mensk lady on molde mon may hir calle,
965   for Gode!
        Hir body watȝ schort and þik,
        Hir buttokeȝ balȝ and brode;
        More lykkerwys on to lyk
        Watȝ þat scho hade on lode.

970   When Gawayn glyȝt on þat gay, þat graciously loked,
        Wyth leue laȝt of þe lorde he lent hem aȝaynes.
        Þe alder he haylses, heldande ful lowe;
        Þe loueloker he lappeȝ a lyttel in armeȝ,
        He kysses hir comlyly, and knyȝtly he meleȝ.
975   Þay kallen hym of aquoyntaunce, and he hit quyk askeȝ
        To be her seruaunt sothly, if hemself lyked.
        Þay tan hym bytwene hem, wyth talkyng hym leden
        To chambre, to chemné, and chefly þay asken
        Spyceȝ, þat vnsparely men speded hom to bryng,
980   And þe wynnelych wyne þerwith vche tyme.
        Þe lorde luflych aloft lepeȝ ful ofte,
        Mynned merthe to be made vpon mony syþeȝ,
        Hent heȝly of his hode, and on a spere henged,
        And wayned hom to wynne þe worchip þerof,
985   Þat most myrþe myȝt meue þat Crystenmas whyle;
        "And I schal fonde, bi my fayth, to fylter wyth þe best
        Er me wont þe wede, with help of my frendeȝ."
        Þus wyth laȝande loteȝ þe lorde hit tayt makeȝ,
        For to glade Sir Gawayn with gomneȝ in halle
990   þat nyȝt,
        Til þat hit watȝ tyme
        Þe lord comaundet lyȝt;

72

And those were sour to see   and exceedingly bleared;
An honorable lady on earth   men may her call,
965   For God!
        Her body was short and thick,
        Her buttocks big and broad;
        A more luscious one to pick
        Was she with whom she trod.

970   When Gawain glanced on that gay,   that graciously looked,
       With leave allowed by the lord   the ladies he greets.
       The elder he hails,   bowing full low;
       The more lovely he laps   a little in arms,
       He kisses her comely,   and knightly he speaks.
975   They request his acquaintance,   and he quickly asks
       To be their servant soothly,   if they so pleased.
       They take him between them,   with talking him lead
       To chamber, to chimney,   and cheerfully order
       Spices, that unsparingly   men sped them to bring,
980   And the excellent wine   there-with each time.
       The lord lively aloft   leaps full oft,
       Commanded mirth to be made   many a time,
       Hastily doffed his hood,   and on a spear hanged it,
       And waved them to win   the worship there-of,
985   Who most mirth might move   that Christmas time;
       "And I shall try, by my faith,   to contend with the best
       Lest I lose the hood,   with help of my friends."
       Thus with laughing speech   the lord makes merry,
       For to gladden Sir Gawain   with games in hall
990   That night,
        Till it was late eve;
        The lord commanded light;

Sir Gawen his leue con nyme
And to his bed hym di3t.

995   On þe morne, as vch mon myne3 þat tyme
Þat Dry3tyn for oure destyné to de3e watz borne,
Wele waxe3 in vche a won in worlde for His sake;
So did hit þere on þat day þur3 dayntés mony:
Boþe at mes and at mele messes ful quaynt
1000   Derf men vpon dece drest of þe best.
Þe olde auncian wyf he3est ho sytte3,
Þe lorde lufly her by lent, as I trowe;
Gawan and þe gay burde togeder þay seten,
Euen inmydde3, as þe messe metely come,
1005   And syþen þur3 al þe sale as hem best semed;
Bi vche grome at his degré grayþely watz serued
Þer watz mete, þer watz myrþe, þer watz much ioye,
Þat for to telle þerof hit me tene were,
And to poynte hit 3et I pyned me parauenture.
1010   Bot 3et I wot þat Wawen and þe wale burde
Such comfort of her compaynye ca3ten togeder
Þur3 her dere dalyaunce of her derne worde3,
Wyth clene cortays carp closed fro fylþe,
Þat hor play watz passande vche prynce gomen,
1015   in vayres.
     Trumpe3 and nakerys,
     Much pypyng þer repayres;
     Vche mon tented hys,
     And þay two tented þayres.

1020   Much dut watz þer dryuen þat day and þat oþer,
And þe þryd as þro þronge in þerafter;

Sir Gawain takes his leave,
And then to bed aright.

995 On the morn, as each man   remembers that time
     That Dear God for our destiny   to die was born,
     Joy waxes in each dwelling   in world for His sake;
     So did it there on that day   through dainties many:
     Both at breakfast and at dinner   dishes full elaborate;
1000 Doughty men upon dais   dined on the best;
     The old ancient wife   highest she sits,
     The lord attentively by her lounged,   as I believe;
     Gawain and the gay lady   together they sat,
     Right in the middle,   where the meals first come,
1005 And are then served to all,   as to them best seemed;
     Each good man, by his degree,   graciously was served.
     There were meals, there was mirth,   there was much joy,
     That for to tell there-of   would be trouble for me,
     And to compose it just now   pained me indeed.
1010 But yet I know well that Wawain   and the winsome lady
     Such comfort of their company   caught together
     Through the dear dalliance   of their secret words,
     With clean courteous discourse   clear from filth,
     And their play surpassed   each princely game,
1015   And fair.
          Trumpets and drummers the best.
          Much piping there repairs;
          Each man tends his business,
          And those two tended theirs.

1020 Much delight was there driven   that day and the next,
     And the third as delightful   thrust in there-after;

Þe ioye of Sayn Jone3 Day wat3 gentyle to here,

And wat3 þe last of þe layk, leude3 þer þo3ten.

Þer wer gestes to go vpon þe gray morne,

1025   Forþy wonderly þay woke, and þe wyn dronken,

Daunsed ful dre3ly wyth dere carole3.

At þe last, when hit wat3 late, þay lachen her leue,

Vchon to wende on his way þat wat3 wy3e stronge.

Gawan gef hym god day, þe godmon hym lachche3,

1030   Ledes hym to his awen chambre, þe chymné bysyde,

And þere he dra3e3 hym on dry3e, and derely hym þonkke3

Of þe wynne worschip þat he hym wayued hade,

As to honour his hous on þat hy3e tyde,

And enbelyse his bur3 with his bele chere:

1035   "Iwysse sir, quyl I leue, me worþe3 þe better

Þat Gawayn hat3 ben my gest at Godde3 awen fest."

"Grant merci, sir," quoþ Gawayn, "in god fayth hit is yowre3,

Al þe honour is your awen; þe He3e Kyng yow 3elde!

And I am wy3e at your wylle to worch youre hest,

1040   As I am halden þerto, in hy3e and in lo3e,

        bi ri3t."

      Þe lorde fast can hym payne

      To holde lenger þe kny3t;

      To hym answare3 Gawayn

1045   Bi non way þat he my3t.

Then frayned þe freke ful fayre at himseluen

Quat derue dede had hym dryuen at þat dere tyme

So kenly fro þe kynge3 kourt to kayre al his one,

Er þe halidaye3 holly were halet out of toun.

The joy of Saint John's Day   was gentle to hear,
And was the last of the feasting,   liegemen there thought.
There were guests to go   upon the gray morn,
1025   Therefore long they stayed awake,   and the wine drank,
Danced all unceasingly   with dear carols.
At the last, when it was late,   they took their leave,
Each one to wend on his way   that was a guest warrior.
Gawain gave him good day,   the good man him grabs,
1030   Leads him to his own chamber,   the chimney beside,
And there he draws him aside,   and dearly him thanks
For the noble worship   that he had shown him,
As to honor his house   on that high season,
And embellish his burg   with his buoyant good cheer:
1035   "Indeed sir, while I live,   I will be the better
That Gawain has been my guest   at God's own feast."
"Great thanks, sir," quoth Gawain,   "in good faith it is yours;
All the honor is your own;   may the High King reward you!
And I am warrior at your will   to work your command,
1040   As I am beholden there-to,   in high and in low,
         By right."
              The lord fast did him strain
              To hold longer that knight;
              To him answers Gawain
1045   That in no way he might.

Then asked the fighter   full fair of himself
What doughty deed had him driven   at that dear time
So keenly from the king's court   to canter all alone,
Ere the holidays wholly   were hurried out of town.

1050 "For soþe, sir," quoþ þe segge, "3e sayn bot þe trawþe,
A he3e ernde and a hasty me hade fro þo wone3,
For I am sumned myselfe to sech to a place,
I ne wot in worlde whederwarde to wende hit to fynde.
I nolde bot if I hit negh my3t on Nw 3eres morne
1055 For alle þe londe inwyth Logres, so me oure Lorde help!
Forþy, sir, þis enquest I require yow here,
Þat 3e me telle with trawþe if euer 3e tale herde
Of þe Grene Chapel, quere hit on grounde stonde3,
And of þe kny3t þat hit kepes, of colour of grene.
1060 Þer wat3 stabled bi statut a steuen vus bytwene
To mete þat mon at þat mere, 3if I my3t last;
And of þat ilk Nw 3ere bot neked now wonte3,
And I wolde loke on þat lede, if God me let wolde,
Gladloker, bi Godde3 sun, þen any god welde!
1065 Forþi, iwysse, bi yowre wylle, wende me bihoues,
Naf I now to busy bot bare þre daye3,
And me als fayn to falle feye as fayly of myyn ernde."
Þenne la3ande quoþ þe lorde, "Now leng þe byhoues,
For I schal teche yow to þat terme bi þe tyme3 ende,
1070 Þe Grene Chapayle vpon grounde greue yow no more;
Bot 3e schal be in yowre bed, burne, at þyn ese;
Quyle forth daye3, and ferk on þe fyrst of þe 3ere,
And cum to þat merk at mydmorn, to make quat yow like3
in spenne;
1075 Dowelle3 whyle New 3eres daye,
And rys, and rayke3 þenne.
Mon schal yow sette in waye;
Hit is not two myle henne."

1050   "For sooth, sir," quoth the stalwart,   "ye say but the truth,
A high errand and an important   haled me from home,
For I myself am summoned   to search for a place,
I know not in this world which way   to wend to find it.
I want nothing but to be nigh it   on New Year's morn.

1055   For all the land within Logres,   so help me Our Lord!
Therefore, sir, this request   I require of you here,
That ye me tell with truth   if ever ye tale heard
Of the Green Chapel,   where it on ground stands,
And of the knight that it keeps,   of color of green.

1060   There was set by agreement   a day we arranged
To meet that man at that landmark,   if I might last;
And of that same New Year   but little now lacks,
And I would look on that lad,   if God would let me,
More gladly, by God's Son,   than any good wield!

1065   Therefore, indeed, with your permission,   to wend me behooves.
Nor have I now to be busy   but bare three days,
And I as eager to fall dead   as fail of mine errand."
Then laughing quoth the lord,   "Now linger thee behooves,
For I shall teach you to that place   by the time's end,

1070   Let the Green Chapel upon ground   grieve you no more;
And ye shall be in your bed,   brave, at thine ease;
Wile forth the days, and fare   on the first of the year,
And come to that place at midmorning,   as you please
        In defense;

1075   Dwell until New Year's day,
       And rise, and ride thence.
       We shall set you on the way;
       It is not two miles hence."

Þenne watȝ Gawan ful glad, and gomenly he laȝed:

1080 "Now I þonk yow þryuandely þurȝ alle oþer þynge.
Now acheued is my chaunce, I schal at your wylle
Dowelle, and elleȝ do quat ȝe demen."
Þenne sesed hym þe syre and set hym bysyde,
Let þe ladieȝ be fette to lyke hem þe better.

1085 Þer watȝ seme solace by hemself stille;
Þe lorde let for luf loteȝ so myry,
As wyȝ þat wolde of his wyte, ne wyst quat he myȝt.
Þenne he carped to þe knyȝt, criande loude,
"Ȝe han demed to do þe dede þat I bidde;

1090 Wyl ȝe halde þis hes here at þys oneȝ?"
"Ȝe, sir, for soþe," sayd þe segge trwe,
"Whyl I byde in yowre bore, be bayn to yowre hest."
"For ȝe haf trauayled," quoþ þe tulk, "towen
fro ferre,
And syþen waked me wyth, ȝe arn not wel waryst

1095 Nauþer of sostnaunce ne of slepe, soþly I knowe;
Ȝe schal lenge in your lofte, and lyȝe in your ese
To-morn quyle þe messequyle, and to mete wende
When ȝe wyl, wyth my wyf, þat wyth yow schal sitte
And comfort yow with compayny, til I to cort torne;

1100 ȝe lende,
And I schal erly ryse;
On huntyng wyl I wende."
Gauayn granteȝ alle þyse,
Hym heldande, as þe hende.

1105 "Ȝet firre," quoþ þe freke, "a forwarde we make:
Quat-so-euer I wynne in þe wod hit worþeȝ to youreȝ;
And quat chek so ȝe acheue chaunge me þerforne.

Then was Gawain full glad,   and gleefully he laughed:
1080   "Now I thank you abundantly   over all other things.
Now achieved is my quest!   I shall at your will
Dwell, and else do   whatever ye decide."
Then the sire seized him   and sat him beside,
Let the ladies be fetched   to please them the better.
1085   There was seemly pleasure,   in privacy by themselves;
The lord used for love   language so merry,
Like a warrior that went out of his wit,   nor knew what he did.
Then he called to the knight,   crying loud,
"Ye have decided to do   the deed that I bid;
1090   Will ye hold this promise   here for this once?"
"Yea, sir, for sooth,"   said the stalwart true,
"While I bide in your burg,   I am bound to your command."
"For ye have travelled," quoth the true knight,   "a trip from
                                                              so far,
And then stayed up late with me;   ye are not well restored,
1095   Neither of sustenance nor of sleep,   soothly I know;
Ye shall linger in your loft,   and lie in your ease
Tomorrow during the mass-time,   and to meal wend
When ye will, with my wife,   that with you shall sit
And comfort you with company,   till I to court return;
1100   Linger herein;
           And I shall early rise;
           On hunting will I wend."
       Gawain grants this likewise,
       Holding him his friend.

1105   "Yet further," quoth that fighter,   "first let's agree:
Whatsoever I win in the wood   will be yours;
And what ye achieve here   exchange it with me for that.

81

Swete, swap we so, sware with trawþe,
Queþer, leude, so lymp, lere oþer better."
1110 "Bi God," quoþ Gawayn þe gode, "I grant þertylle,
And þat yow lyst for to layke, lef hit me þynkes."
"Who bryngeȝ vus þis beuerage, þis bargayn is maked."
So sayde þe lorde of þat lede; þay laȝed vchone,
Þay dronken and daylyeden and dalten vntyȝtel,
1115 Þise lordeȝ and ladyeȝ, quyle þat hem lyked;
And syþen with Frenkysch fare and fele fayre loteȝ
Þay stoden and stemed and stylly speken,
Kysten ful comlyly and kaȝten her leue.
With mony leude ful lyȝt and lemande torches
1120 Vche burne to his bed watȝ broȝt at þe laste,
        ful softe.
    To bed ȝet er þay ȝede,
    Recorded couenaunteȝ ofte;
    Þe olde lorde of þat leude
1125 Cowþe wel halde layk alofte.

Sweet, swap we so,   swear with truth,

Whatever, liegemen, so befalls,   loss or gain."

1110   "By God," quoth Gawain the good,   "I grant that,

And that you like such amusements,   seems laudable to me."

"Let someone bring us this beverage;   this bargain is made."

So said the lord of that land;   they laughed each one,

They drank, and dallied,   and dealt unrestrained,

1115   These lords and ladies,   while they pleased;

And then in the French fashion   and many fair words

They stood and stayed   and softly spoke,

Kissed full comely   and caught their leave.

By many liegemen with light   and gleaming torches

1120   Each brave to his bed   was brought at the last

            Full soft.

        To bed yet ere they wend,

        They repeated covenants oft;

        The old lord of that land

1125   Could well hold play aloft.

III

Ful erly bifore þe day þe folk vprysen,
Gestes þat go wolde hor gromeȝ þay calden,
And þay busken vp bilyue blonkkeȝ to sadel,
Tyffen her takles, trussen her males,

1130   Richen hem þe rychest, to ryde alle arayde;
Lepen vp lyȝtly, lachen her brydeles,
Vche wyȝe on his way þer hym wel lyked.
Þe leue lorde of þe londe watȝ not þe last
Arayed for þe rydyng, with renkkeȝ ful mony;

1135   Ete a sop hastyly, when he hade herde masse,
With bugle to bent-felde he buskeȝ bylyue.
By þat any daylyȝt lemed vpon erþe
He with his haþeles on hyȝe horsses weren.
Þenne þise cacheres þat couþe cowpled hor houndeȝ,

1140   Vnclosed þe kenel dore and calde hem þeroute,
Blwe bygly in bugleȝ þre bare mote;
Braches bayed þerfore and breme noyse maked;
And þay chastysed and charred on chasyng þat went,
A hundreth of hunteres, as I haf herde telle,

1145   of þe best.
    To trystors vewters ȝod,
    Couples huntes of kest;
    Þer ros for blasteȝ gode
    Gret rurd in þat forest.

1150   At þe fyrst quethe of þe quest quaked þe wylde;
Der drof in þe dale, doted for drede,
Hiȝed to þe hyȝe, bot heterly þay were
Restayed with þe stablye, þat stoutly ascryed.
Þay let þe hertteȝ haf þe gate, with þe hyȝe hedes,

Full early before the day   the folk get up,
Guests that would go   called their grooms,
And they bustle up busily   broncos to saddle,
Tighten their tackle,   truss up their bags,
1130   The richest ready themselves   to ride all arrayed;
They leap up lightly,   lay hold of their bridles,
Each warrior on his way   where he well pleased.
The lively lord of the land   was not the last
Arrayed for the riding,   with riders full many;
1135   Had a snack hastily,   when he had heard mass,
With bugle to the field   he briskly bounds.
Before any daylight   gleamed upon earth
He with his horsemen   on high horses mounted.
Then these crafty handlers   coupled hounds in pairs,
1140   Unclosed the kennel door   and called them there-out,
Blew boldly in bugles   three long notes;
Big hounds bayed there-at   and brave noise made;
Handlers whipped and turned back   those on false scents,
A hundred of hunters,   as I have heard tell,
1145   Of the best.
          To their stations handlers strode;
          Leashes huntsmen off cast;
          There rose for horn-blasts good
          Great noise in that forest.

1150   At the first sound of the quest   quaked wild beasts;
Deer drove through the dale,   doddered for dread,
Hied to the heights,   but hurriedly they were
Restrained by the beaters,   that sternly shouted.
They let the harts pass by,   with their high horns,

1155 Þe breme bukkeȝ also with hor brode paumeȝ;
For þe fre lorde hade defende in fermysoun tyme
Þat þer schulde no mon meue to þe male dere.
Þe hindeȝ were halden in with "hay!" and "war!"
Þe does dryuen with gret dyn to þe depe sladeȝ;
1160 Þer myȝt mon se, as þay slypte, slentyng of arwes:
At vche wende vnder wande wapped a flone
Þat bigly bote on þe broun with ful brode hedeȝ.
What! þay brayen, and bleden, bi bonkkeȝ þay deȝen,
And ay rachches in a res radly hem folȝes,
1165 Huntereȝ wyth hyȝe horne hasted hem after
Wyth such a crakkande kry as klyffes haden brusten.
What wylde so atwaped wyȝes þat schotten
Watȝ al toraced and rent at þe resayt,
Bi þay were tened at þe hyȝe and taysed to þe wattreȝ;
1170 Þe ledeȝ were so lerned at þe loȝe trysteres,
And þe grehoundeȝ so grete, þat geten hem bylyue
And hem tofylched, as fast as frekeȝ myȝt loke,
        þer ryȝt.
        Þe lorde for blys abloy
1175   Ful oft con launce and lyȝt,
        And drof þat day wyth joy
        Thus to þe derk nyȝt.

Þus laykeȝ þis lorde by lynde-wodeȝ eueȝ,
And Gawayn þe god mon in gay bed lygeȝ,
1180 Lurkkeȝ quyl þe daylyȝt lemed on þe wowes,
Vnder couertour ful clere, cortyned aboute;
And as in slomeryng he slode, sleȝly he herde
A littel dyn at his dor, and dernly vpon;

88

1155 The brave bucks also with their broad antlers;
   For the fine lord had forbidden in closed-season time
   That any man there should move on the male deer.
   The hinds were held in with "hey!" and "be ware!"
   The does driven with great din to the deep valley;
1160 There might man see, as they slipped by, slanting arrows:
   At each path in the woods an arrow whipped by
   That boldly bit on the brown with broad arrowheads.
   Hey! they bellow, and bleed, by banks they die,
   And ever bloodhounds in a rush rapidly them follow;
1165 Hunters with high horns hastened them after
   With such a crackling cry as if cliffs had burst.
   Whatever wild that escaped the warriors who shot
   Dogs pulled down and tore at the hunt station,
   When they were harassed on hills and harried to the waters;
1170 The lads were so well trained at the low hunt-stations,
   And the greyhounds so great, that got them quickly
   And filched them faster than fighters could look
     There aright.
    The lord his bliss to enjoy
1175   Did oft race ahead and alight,
    And drove that day with joy
    Thus to the dark night.

   Thus gallops this lord by a linden-wood's edges,
   And Gawain the good man in gay bed lies,
1180 Lurks while the daylight gleamed on the walls,
   Under glowing coverings, curtained about;
   And as in slumbering he slid, slightly he heard
   A little din at his door, and stealthily done;

And he heueʒ vp his hed out of þe cloþes,

1185   A corner of þe cortyn he caʒt vp a lyttel,

And wayteʒ warly þiderwarde quat hit be myʒt.

Hit watʒ þe ladi, loflyest to beholde,

Þat droʒ þe dor after hir ful dernly and stylle,

And boʒed towarde þe bed; and þe burne schamed,

1190   And layde hym doun lystyly, and let as he slepte;

And ho stepped stilly and stel to his bedde,

Kest vp þe cortyn and creped withinne,

And set hir ful softly on þe bed-syde,

And lenged þere selly longe to loke quen he wakened.

1195   Þe lede lay lurked a ful longe quyle,

Compast in his concience to quat þat cace myʒt

Meue oþer amount; to meruayle hym þoʒt,

Bot ʒet he sayde in hymself, "More semly hit were

To aspye wyth my spelle in space quat ho wolde."

1200   Þen he wakenede, and wroth, and to hir warde torned,

And vnlouked his yʒe-lyddeʒ, and let as hym wondered,

And sayned hym, as bi his saʒe þe sauer to worthe,

        with hande.

    Wyth chynne and cheke ful swete,

1205   Boþe quit and red in blande;

    Ful lufly con ho lete

    Wyth lyppeʒ smal laʒande.

"God moroun, Sir Gawayn," sayde þat gay lady,

"ʒe ar a sleper vnslyʒe, þat mon may slyde hider;

1210   Now ar ʒe tan as-tyt! Bot true vus may schape:

I schal bynde yow in your bedde, þat be ʒe trayst":

Al laʒande þe lady lanced þo bourdeʒ.

"Goud moroun, gay," quoþ Gawayn þe blyþe,

And he lifts up his head   out of the bedclothes,
1185   A corner of the curtain   he caught up a little,
And looks warily thitherward   what it might be.
It was the lady,   loveliest to behold,
That drew the door after her,   full stealthy and still,
And moved toward the bed;   and the brave shammed,
1190   And laid him down cautiously,   and let on that he slept;
And she stepped stilly   and stole to his bed,
Cast up the curtain   and crept within,
And set her full softly   on the bed-side,
And lingered there very long   to look when he wakened.
1195   The lad lay lurking   a full long while,
Considered in his conscience   to what that case might
Move or amount to;   a marvel he thought,
But yet he said in himself,   "More seemly it would be
To inquire with my speech   openly what she wants."
1200   Then he awakened, and twisted,   and toward her turned,
And unlocked his eye-lids,   and let on that he wondered,
And signed himself, as if by his speech   the safer to be,
            With hand.
        With chin and cheek full sweet,
1205   .   Both white and red in blend;
        Full lovingly did she him greet
        With small laughing lips, as a friend.

"Good morrow, Sir Gawain,"   said that gay lady,
"Ye are not a sly sleeper,   that one may slip hither;
1210   Now are ye taken in a trice!   But a truce we may shape:
I shall bind you in your bed,   that be ye sure":
All laughing the lady   launched those jests.
"Good morrow, gay,"   quoth Gawain the blithe,

"Me schal worþe at your wille, and þat me wel lykeȝ,
1215   For I ȝelde me ȝederly, and ȝeȝe after grace,
And þat is þe best, be my dome, for me byhoueȝ nede":
And þus he bourded aȝayn with mony a blyþe laȝter;
"Bot wolde ȝe, lady louely, þen leue me grante,
And deprece your prysoun, and pray hym to ryse,
1220   I wolde boȝe of þis bed, and busk me better;
I schulde keuer þe more comfort to karp yow wyth."
"Nay for soþe, beau sir," sayd þat swete,
"Ȝe schal not rise of your bedde; I rych yow better;
I schal happe yow here þat oþer half als,
1225   And syþen karp wyth my knyȝt þat I kaȝt haue;
For I wene wel, iwysse, Sir Wowen ȝe are,
Þat alle þe worlde worchipeȝ quere-so ȝe ride;
Your honour, your hendelayk is hendely praysed
With lordeȝ, wyth ladyes, with alle þat lyf bere.
1230   And now ȝe ar here, iwysse, and we bot oure one;
My lorde and his ledeȝ ar on lenþe faren,
Oþer burneȝ in her bedde, and my burdeȝ als,
Þe dor drawen and dit with a derf haspe;
And syþen I haue in þis hous hym þat al lykeȝ,
1235   I schal ware my whyle wel, quyl hit lasteȝ,
              with tale.
          Ȝe ar welcum to my cors,
          Yowre awen won to wale;
          Me behoueȝ of fyne force
1240   Your seruaunt be, and schale."

"In god fayth," quoþ Gawayn, "gayn hit me þynkkeȝ,
Þaȝ I be not now he þat ȝe of speken
To reche to such reuerence as ȝe reherce here

"I shall work at your will,   and that I well like,
1215   For I yield me utterly,   and yearn for grace,
And that is best, as I believe,   for I am obliged by need."
And thus he jested in turn   with many a jolly laugh:
"But would ye, lady lovely,   then grant me leave,
And parole your prisoner,   and pray him to rise,
1220   I would bound from this bed,   and prepare me better;
I should have the more comfort   to converse with you."
"Nay for sooth, beau sir,"   said that sweet,
"Ye shall not rise from your bed;   I will arrange things better;
I shall lock you here,   on that other side also,
1225   And then converse with my knight   that I have caught;
For I well know, indeed,   Sir Wawain ye are,
That all the world worships   where-ever ye ride;
Your honor, your courtesy,   is courteously praised
By lords, by ladies,   by all that bear life.
1230   And now ye are here, indeed,   and we but ourselves alone;
My lord and his lads   are a long way off,
Other braves in their beds,   and my bonnie maids as well,
The door drawn and locked   with a doughty hasp;
And since I have in this house   him that all pleases,
1235   I shall wile my while well,   while it lasts,
                With tale.
        You are welcome to my body,
        Your own will to avail;
        It behooves me of pure force
1240   Your servant be, and I shall."

"In good faith," quoth Gawain,   "gainful it seems to me,
Though I be not now he   of whom ye speak
To reach such reverence   as ye rehearse here

I am wyȝe vnworþy, I wot wel myseluen.

1245   Bi God, I were glad, and yow god þoȝt,
At saȝe oþer at seruyce þat I sette myȝt
To þe plesaunce of your prys; hit were a pure ioye."
"In god fayth, Sir Gawayn," quoþ þe gay lady,
"Þe prys and þe prowes þat pleseȝ al oþer,

1250   If I hit lakked oþer set at lyȝt, hit were littel daynté;
Bot hit ar ladyes innoȝe þat leuer wer nowþe
Haf þe, hende, in hor holde, as I þe habbe here,
To daly with derely your daynté wordeȝ,
Keuer hem comfort and colen her careȝ,

1255   Þen much of þe garysoun oþer golde þat þay hauen.
Bot I louue þat ilk Lorde þat þe lyfte haldeȝ,
I haf hit holly in my honde þat al desyres,
       þurȝe grace."
    Scho made hym so gret chere,

1260   Þat watȝ so fayr of face;
    Þe knyȝt with speches skere
    Answared to vche a cace.

"Madame," quoth the myry man, "Mary yow ȝelde,
For I haf founden, in god fayth, yowre fraunchis nobele

1265   And oþer ful much of oþer folk fongen bi hor dedeȝ,
Bot þe daynté þat þay delen, for my disert nys euen;
Hit is þe worchyp of yourself, þat noȝt bot wel conneȝ."
"Bi Mary," quoþ þe menskful, "me þynk hit an oþer;
For were I worth al þe wone of wymmen alyue,

1270   And al þe wele of þe worlde were in my honde,
And I schulde chepen and chose to cheue me a lorde,
For þe costes þat I haf knowen vpon þe, knyȝt, here,

94

I am a warrior unworthy,   I know well myself.
1245   By God, I would be glad,   and if it seemed good to you,
That my speech or my service   I might set
To the pleasure of your self;   it would be a pure joy."
"In good faith, Sir Gawain,"   quoth the gay lady,
"The praise and the prowess   that pleases all others,
1250   If I blamed it or slighted its value,   it would be little pleasure;
But there are many ladies   that would rather now
Have thee, handsome, in their hold,   as I have thee here,
Dearly to dally   with your dainty words,
Cover them with comfort   and cool their cares,
1255   Than much of the goods   or gold that they have.
But as I love that same Lord   That lifts up the heavens,
I have it wholly in my hand   that all desire,
          Through grace."
      She made him much good cheer,
1260   Who was so fair of face;
      The knight with speeches pure
      Answered to every case.

"Madame," quoth the merry man,   "May Mary reward you,
For I have found, in good faith,   your free nobility,
1265   And full many from other folk   find praise for their deeds,
But the honor that they do to me,   does not equal my deserts;
It is the worship of yourself,   who know nothing but good."
"By Mary," quoth the mannerly,   "To me it seems otherwise;
For were I worth all the multitude   of women alive,
1270   And all the wealth of the world   were in my hand,
And I should shop and choose   to purchase me a lord,
For the qualities that I have known,   in thee, knight, here,

Of bewté and debonerté and blyþe semblaunt,
And þat I haf er herkkened and halde hit here trwee,
1275　Þer schulde no freke vpon folde bifore yow be chosen."
"Iwysse, worþy," quoþ þe wyӡe, "ӡe haf waled wel better;
Bot I am proude of þe prys þat ӡe put on me,
And, soberly your seruaunt, my souerayn I holde yow,
And yowre knyӡt I becom, and Kryst yow foryelde."
1280　Þus þay meled of muchquat til mydmorn paste,
And ay þe lady let lyk as hym loued mych;
Þe freke ferde with defence, and feted ful fayre.
"Þaӡ I were burde brytӡest," þe burde in mynde hade,
"Þe lasse luf in his lode for lur þat he soӡt
1285　　　　boute hone,
Þe dunte þat schulde hym deue,
And nedeӡ hit most be done."
Þe lady þenn spek of leue,
He granted hir ful sone.

1290　Þenne ho gef hym god day, and wyth a glent laӡed,
And as ho stod, ho stonyed hym wyth ful storwordeӡ:
"Now He þat spedeӡ vche spech þis disport ӡelde yow!
Bot þat ӡe be Gawan, hit gotӡ in mynde."
"Querfore?" quoþ þe freke, and freschly he askeӡ,
1295　Ferde lest he hade fayled in fourme of his castes;
Bot þe burde hym blessed, and "Bi þis skyl" sayde:
"So god as Gawayn gaynly is halden,
And cortaysye is closed so clene in hymseluen,
Couth not lyӡtly haf lenged so long wyth a lady,
1300　Bot he had craued a cosse, bi his courtaysye,
Bi sum towch of summe tryfle at sum taleӡ ende."

Of beauty and good manners   and blithe demeanor,
And what I have ere heard   and hold it here true,

1275   There should no fighter upon field   before you be chosen."
"Indeed, worthy," quoth the warrior,   "ye have chosen better;
But I am proud of the price   that ye put on me,
And, soberly your servant,   my sovereign I hold you,
And your knight I become,   and Christ you reward."

1280   Thus they talked of this and that   till midmorning passed,
And ever the lady let on   that she him loved much;
The fighter fared with defense,   and feigned full fair.
"Though I were the brightest,"   the beauty had in mind,
"The less room for love in his luggage   till his journey

1285   Is begun,
        For the dint that shall him grieve,
        And now it must be done."
        The lady then spoke of leave;
        He granted it at once

1290   Then she gave him good day,   and with a glance laughed,
And as she stood, she astonished him   with full strong words:
"Now He that sustains each speech   for this sport reward you!
But that ye be Gawain,   it goes against what I know."
"Wherefore?" quoth the fighter,   and quickly he asks,

1295   Feared lest he had failed   in the form of his speech;
But the lady him blessed,   and said "For this reason:
One so good as Gawain   is rightly considered,
And courtesy enclosed   so completely in himself,
Could not easily have lingered   so long with a lady,

1300   But he had craved a kiss,   by his courtesy,
By some touch of some trifle   at some tale's end."

Þen quoþ Wowen: "Iwysse, worþe as yow lykeȝ;
I schal kysse at your comaundement, as a knyȝt falleȝ,
And fire, lest he displese yow, so plede hit no more."

1305 Ho comes nerre with þat, and cacheȝ hym in armeȝ,
Louteȝ luflych adoun and þe leude kysseȝ.
Þay comly bykennen to Kryst ayþer oþer;
Ho dos hir forth at þe dore withouten dyn more,
And he ryches hym to ryse and rapes hym sone,

1310 Clepes to his chamberlayn, choses his wede,
Boȝeȝ forth, quen he watȝ boun, blyþely to masse;
And þenne he meued to his mete þat menskly hym keped,
And made myry al day, til þe mone rysed,
            with game.

1315   Watȝ neuer freke fayrer fonge
          Bitwene two so dyngne dame,
          Þe alder and þe ȝonge;
          Much solace set þay same.

And ay þe lorde of þe londe is lent on his gamneȝ,

1320 To hunt in holteȝ and heþe at hyndeȝ barayne;
Such a sowme he þer slowe bi þat þe sunne heldet,
Of dos and of oþer dere, to deme were wonder.
Þenne fersly þay flokked in folk at þe laste,
And quykly of þe quelled dere a querré þay maked,

1325 Þe best boȝed þerto with burneȝ innoghe,
Gedered þe grattest of gres þat þer were,
And didden hem derely vndo as þe dede askeȝ;
Serched hem at þe asay summe þat þer were;
Two fyngeres þay fonde of þe fowlest of alle.

Then quoth Wawain: "Indeed,   work as you like;
I shall kiss at your commandment,   as a knight should,
And more, lest he displease you,   so plead it no more."

1305   She comes nearer with that,   and catches him in arms,
Bows lovingly down   and the liegeman kisses.
Either the other they courteously   entrust to Christ.
She goes forth to the door   without din more,
And he prepares him to rise   and rushes him soon,

1310   Calls to his servant,   selects his clothes,
Bounds forth, when he was ready,   blithely to mass;
And then he moved to his meal   that worthily him awaited,
And made merry all day,   till the moon rose,
                With game.

1315   Was never fair fighter so well
            Received by such worthy dames,
            The elder and the belle;
            Much pleasure and ever the same.

And ever the lord of the land   is intent on his game,

1320   To hunt in woods and heath   at barren hinds;
Such a sum he there slew   till the sun went down,
Of does and of other deer,   wondrous to declare.
Then fiercely the folk   flocked in at the last,
And quickly of the quelled deer,   their quarry, made a pile,

1325   The best bounded there-to   with many braves,
Gathered the greatest in grease   that were there,
And had them carefully cut open,   as the art requires;
Searched out at the assessment   some that were there;
Two fingers of fat they found   in the least of their quarry.

1330   Syþen þay slyt þe slot, sesed þe erber,
           Schaued wyth a scharp knyf, and þe schyre knitten;
           Syþen rytte þay þe foure lymmes, and rent of þe hyde,
           Þen brek þay þe balé, þe boweleʒ out token
           Lystily for laucyng þe lere of þe knot;
1335   Þay gryped to þe gargulun, and grayþely departed
           Þe wesaunt fro þe wynt-hole, and walt out þe gutteʒ;
           Þen scher þay out þe schuldereʒ with her scharp knyueʒ,
           Haled hem by a lyttel hole to haue hole sydes.
           Siþen britned þay þe brest and brayden hit in twynne,
1340   And eft at þe gargulun bigyneʒ on þenne,
           Ryueʒ hit vp radly ryʒt to þe byʒt,
           Voydeʒ out þe avanters, and verayly þerafter
           Alle þe rymeʒ by þe rybbeʒ radly þay lance;
           So ryde þay of by resoun bi þe rygge boneʒ,
1345   Euenden to þe haunche, þat henged alle samen,
           And heuen hit vp al hole, and hwen hit of þere,
           And þat þay neme for þe noumbles bi nome, as I trowe,
                    bi kynde;
             Bi þe byʒt al of þe þyʒes
1350   Þe lappeʒ þay lance bihynde;
             To hewe hit in two þay hyʒes,
             Bi þe bakbon to vnbynde.

           Boþe þe hede and þe hals þay hwen of þenne,
           And syþen sunder þay þe sydeʒ swyft fro þe chyne,
1355   And þe corbeles fee þay kest in a greue;
           Þenn þurled þay ayþer þik side þurʒ bi þe rybbe,
           And henged þenne ayþer bi hoʒeʒ of þe fourcheʒ.
           Vche freke for his fee, as falleʒ for to haue.

1330   Next they slit the slot of the throat,   seized the stomach,
           Shaved it with a sharp knife,   and the shining flesh knotted;
           Next they ripped off the four legs,   and rent off the hide,
           Then they broke open the belly,   took out the bowels
           Carefully, to avoid loosening,   tied back the flesh;
1335   They proceeded to the throat,   and mannerly parted
           The gullet from the windpipe,   and threw out the guts;
           Then shear they out the shoulders   with their sharp knives,
           Hauled them out by a little hole   to keep the sides whole.
           Next broke they the breast   and pulled it in two,
1340   And then again begins   one at the throat,
           Rips it up quickly   right to the fork,
           Voids out the waste parts,   and verily there-after
           All the membranes by the ribs   rapidly they loosen;
           So correctly they cleaned   the back bones,
1345   All the way to the haunch,   that it hanged all together,
           And they heave it up all whole,   and hew it off there,
           And that they take for "the numbles"   by name, as I believe,
                 Assigned;
              By the thigh-bones they placed
1350   The flesh they loosened behind;
              To hew it in two they haste,
              The backbone to unbind.

           Both the head and the neck   they hew off then,
           And then split they the sides   swiftly from the spine,
1355   And the "crow's share"   they cast in a thicket;
           Then pierced they through   both thick sides by the rib,
           And hanged them both   by hocks of the legs.
           Each fighter has his fee,   as befits him to have.

Vpon a felle of þe fayre best fede þay þayr houndes

1360 Wyth þe lyuer and þe lyȝteȝ, þe leþer of þe pauncheȝ,
And bred baþed in blod blende þeramongeȝ.
Baldely þay blw prys, bayed þayr rachcheȝ,
Syþen fonge þay her flesche, folden to home,
Strakande ful stoutly mony stif moteȝ.

1365 Bi þat þe daylyȝt watȝ done þe doutheȝ watȝ al wonen
Into þe comly castel, þer þe knyȝt bideȝ
ful stille,
Wyth blys and bryȝt fyr bette.
Þe lorde is comen þertylle;

1370 When Gawayn wyth hym mette
Þer watȝ bot wele at wylle.

Thenne comaunded þe lorde in þat sale to samen alle þe
meny.
Boþe þe ladyes on loghe to lyȝt with her burdes.
Bifore alle þe folk on þe flette, frekeȝ he beddeȝ

1375 Verayly his venysoun to fech hym byforne,
And al godly in gomen Gawayn he called,
Techeȝ hym to þe tayles of ful tayt bestes,
Scheweȝ hym þe schyree grece schorne vpon rybbes.
"How payeȝ yow þis play? Haf I prys wonnen?

1380 Haue I þryuandely þonk þurȝ my craft serued?"
"Ȝe iwysse," quoþ þat oþer wyȝe, "here is wayth
fayrest
Þat I seȝ þis seuen ȝere in sesoun of wynter."
"And al I gif yow, Gawayn," quoþ þe gome þenne,
"For by acorde of couenaunt ȝe craue hit as your awen."

1385 "Þis is soth," quoþ þe segge, "I say yow þat ilke:
Þat I haf worthyly wonnen þis woneȝ wythinne,

102

Upon a pelt of the fair beast   feed they their hounds

1360   With the liver and the lungs,   the lining of the stomach,
And bread bathed in blood   blended among it.
Boldly horns blew "taken!"   Their hounds bayed.
Then take they their flesh,   fare to home,
Sounding full stoutly   many long notes.

1365   By the time daylight was done   the company was all come
Into the comely castle,   where the knight bides
        Full still,
    With bliss and bright fire heat,
    Comes the lord until

1370   Gawain with him did meet,
    And all was joy at will.

Then commanded the lord in that hall   to gather the
                                        court.
Both the ladies came down   with their lovely maids.
Before all the folk on the floor,   fighters he bids

1375   Verily his venison   to fetch before him him,
And all goodly, in game,   Gawain he called,
Tells him the tally   of beasts taken,
Shows him the shining grease   shorn from the ribs.
"How repay you this play?   Have I the prize won?

1380   Have I well-earned thanks   through my craft deserved?"
"Yea indeed," quoth that other warrior,   "here is the fairest
                                            game
That I have seen this seven year   in season of winter."
"And all I give you, Gawain,"   quoth the gallant then,
"For by accord of our covenant   ye may claim it as your own."

1385   "This is sooth," quoth the stalwart,   "I say you the same:
What I have worthily won   within these walls,

Iwysse with as god wylle hit worþeȝ to youreȝ."
He hasppeȝ his fayre hals his armeȝ wythinne,
And kysses hym as comlyly as he couþe awyse:
1390 "Tas yow þere my cheuicaunce, I cheued no more;
I wowche hit saf fynly, þaȝ feler hit were."
"Hit is god," quoþ þe godmon, "grant mercy þerfore.
Hit may be such hit is þe better, and ȝe me breue wolde
Where ȝe wan þis ilk wele bi wytte of yorseluen."
1395 "Þat watȝ not forward," quoþ he, "frayst me no more.
For ȝe haf tan þat yow tydeȝ, trawe non oþer
ȝe mowe."
Þay laȝed, and made hem blyþe
Wyth loteȝ þat were to lowe;
1400 To soper þay ȝede as-swyþe,
Wyth dayntés nwe innowe.

And syþen by þe chymné in chamber þay seten,
Wyȝeȝ þe walle wyn weȝed to hem oft,
And efte in her bourdyng þay bayþen in þe morn
1405 To fylle þe same forwardeȝ þat þay byfore maden:
Wat chaunce so bytydeȝ hor cheuysaunce to chaunge,
What nweȝ so þay nome, at naȝt quen þay metten.
Þay acorded of þe couenaunteȝ byfore þe court alle;
Þe beuerage watȝ broȝt forth in bourde at þat tyme.
1410 Þenne þay louelych leȝten leue at þe last;
Vche burne to his bedde busked bylyue.
Bi þat þe coke hade crowen and cakled bot þryse,
Þe lorde watȝ lopen of his bedde, þe leudeȝ vchone;
So þat þe mete and þe masse watȝ metely delyuered,

Indeed with as good will   it becomes yours."
He clasps his fair neck   within his arms,
And kisses him as courteously   as he knew how:
1390   "Take you there my winnings,   I won no more;
I grant it completely,   and would it were more."
"It is good," quoth the good man,   "great thanks there-for.
It would be the better,   if ye would me declare
Where ye won this same wealth   by wit of yourself."
1395   "That was not agreed," quoth he,   "ask me no more.
For ye have taken what belongs to you;   expect nothing more
      There-by."
          They laughed, and made them blithe
          With words of praise on high;
1400   To supper they swiftly stride,
          Some dainties new to try.

And then by the chimney   in chamber they sat,
Warriors the bright wine   brought to them oft,
And again in their bantering   both agree in the morn
1405   To fulfill the same agreements   that they before made:
Whatever by chance betides,   their winnings to exchange,
Whatever new thing they take,   at night when they met.
They agreed to the covenants   before all the court;
The beverage was brought   to seal the bargain then.
1410   Then they lovingly   took leave at the last;
Each brave to his bed   bounded in haste.
By the time the cock had crowed   and cackled but thrice,
The lord had leaped from his bed,   and each liegeman;
When the meal and the mass   were properly served,

1415   Þe douthe dressed to þe wod, er any day sprenged,
           to chace;
        Heȝ with hunte and horneȝ
        Þurȝ playneȝ þay passe in space.
        Vncoupled among þo þorneȝ
1420   Racheȝ þat ran on race.

Sone þay calle of a quest in a ker syde,
Þe hunt rehayted þe houndeȝ þat hit fyrst mynged;
Wylde wordeȝ hym warp wyth a wrast noyce;
Þe howndeȝ þat hit herde hastid þider swyþe,
1425   And fellen as fast to þe fuyt, fourty at ones;
Þenne such a glauer ande glam of gedered rachcheȝ
Ros, þat þe rochereȝ rungen aboute;
Huntereȝ hem hardened with horne and wyth muthe.
Þen al in a semblé sweyed togeder,
1430   Bitwene a flosche in þat fryth and a foo cragge;
In a knot bi a clyffe, at þe kerre syde,
Þer as þe rogh rocher vnrydely watȝ fallen,
Þay ferden to þe fyndyng, and frekeȝ hem after;
Þay vmbekesten þe knarre and þe knot boþe,
1435   Wyȝeȝ, whyl þay wysten wel wythinne hem hit were.
Þe best þat þer breued watȝ wyth þe blodhoundeȝ.
Þenne þay beten on þe buskeȝ, and bede hym vpryse,
And he vnsoundyly out soȝt seggeȝ ouerþwert;
On þe sellokest swyn swenged out þere,
1440   Long sythen fro þe sounder þat siȝed for olde,
For he watȝ breme, bor alþer-grattest,
Ful grymme quen he gronyed; þenne greued mony,
For þre at þe fyrst þrast he þryȝt to þe erþe,

1415   The company dashed to the wood,   ere any day sprang,
           To the chase;
        Hasting with hunters and horns;
        Through plains they race.
        Uncoupled among those thorns
1420   Hounds that rushed apace.

Soon they call of a quarry   found on a marsh's side,
The hunter urged on the hounds   that found it first;
Wild words they shouted   with a loud noise;
The hounds that heard it   hastened thither swiftly,
1425   And fell fast to the track,   forty at once;
Then such a great barking and din   of gathered hounds
Arose, that the rocky hills   rang all about;
Hunters them heartened   with horn and with mouth.
Then all in a solid pack   swiftly came together,
1430   Between a pool in that forest   and a forbidding crag;
In a cluster by a cliff,   at the marsh's side,
Where the rough rock   in ruins was fallen,
Hounds fared to the find,   and fighters them after;
They searched around the rocky hill   and the summit as well,
1435   Warriors, while they knew well   within there it was.
The best that there bayed   were with the bloodhounds.
Then they beat on the bushes,   and bade him uprise,
And he, disastrously, sought out   stalwarts in his path;
The most splendid swine   swung out there,
1440   Long since from the herd   set apart for age,
For he was brave,   biggest of all boars,
Full grim when he growled;   then grieved many,
For three at the first thrust   he threw to the earth,

And sparred forth good sped boute spyt more.

1445 Þise oþer halowed "Hyghe!" ful hyʒe, and "Hay! Hay!" cryed,
Haden hornez to mouþe, heterly rechated:
Mony watz þe myry mouthe of men and of houndez
Þat buskkez after þis bor with bost and wyth noyse
to quelle.

1450 Ful oft he bydez þe baye,
And maymez þe mute inn melle;
He hurtez of þe houndez, and þay
Ful ʒomerly ʒaule and ʒelle.

Schalkez to schote at hym schowen to þenne,

1455 Haled to hym of her arewez, hitten hym oft;
Bot þe poyntez payred at þe pyth þat pyʒt in his scheldez,
And þe barbez of his browe bite non wolde;
Þaʒ þe schauen schaft schyndered in pecez,
Þe hede hypped aʒayn were-so-euer hit hitte.

1460 Bot quen þe dyntez hym dered of her dryʒe strokez,
Þen, braynwod for bate, on burnez he rasez,
Hurtez hem ful heterly þer he forth hyʒez,
And mony arʒed þerat, and on lyte droʒen.
Bot þe lorde on a lyʒt horce launces hym after,

1465 As burne bolde vpon bent his bugle he blowez,
He rechated, and rode þurʒ ronez ful þyk,
Suande þis wylde swyn til þe sunne schafted.
Þis day wyth þis ilk dede þay dryuen on þis wyse,
Whyle oure luflych lede lys in his bedde,

1470 Gawayn grayþely at home, in gerez ful ryche
of hewe.
Þe lady noʒt forʒate,
Com to hym to salue.

And sprang forth at good speed   despite his harms.

1445 The others shouted "Hurry!" full high,   and "Hey! Hey!" cried,
Had horns to mouth,   heartily sounded "recall":
Many were the merry sounds   of men and of hounds
That bound after this boar   with boast and with noise
       Full fell.

1450   Full oft he bides at bay,
      And maims the pack pell-mell;
      He hurts some hounds, and they
      Full piteously yowl and yell.

Chevaliers to shoot at him   shove forth then,

1455 Have at him with their arrows,   hit him oft;
But the points hitting the shoulder   its strength blunted
And none could bite into   the bristles of his brow;
Though the sharpened shaft   shattered in pieces,
The arrow-head rebounded   where-so-ever it hit.

1460 But when the hits him hurt   with their heavy strokes,
Then, brain-mad for battle,   on braves he rushes,
Hurts them full hatefully   where he forth hastens,
And many feared there-at,   and drew back a little.
But the lord on a lively horse   leaps him after,

1465 And the brave one, bold on the field,   his bugle he blows,
He blew "recall," and rode through   bushes full thick,
Pursuing this wild swine   till the sun settled.
All day with this same deed   they do in this way,
While our lovely lad   lies in his bed,

1470 Gawain gracefully at home,   in garments full rich
       Of hue.
      The lady did not forget,
      To come to him for her due.

Ful erly ho watȝ hym ate

1475 His mode for to remwe.

Ho commes to þe cortyn, and at þe knyȝt totes.
Sir Wawen her welcumed worþy on fyrst,
And ho hym ȝeldeȝ aȝayn ful ȝerne of hir wordeȝ,
Setteȝ hir softly by his syde, and swyþely ho laȝeȝ,
1480 And wyth a luflych loke ho layde hym þyse wordeȝ:
"Sir, ȝif ȝe be Wawen, wonder me þynkkeȝ,
Wyȝe þat is so wel wrast alway to god,
And conneȝ not of compaynye þe costeȝ vndertake,
And if mon kennes yow hom to knowe, ȝe kest hom of your
mynde.
1485 Þou hatȝ forȝeten ȝederly þat ȝisterday I taȝtte
Bi alder-truest token of talk þat I cowþe."
"What is þat?" quoþ þe wyȝe, "Iwysse I wot neuer;
If hit be sothe þat ȝe breue, þe blame is myn awen."
"ȝet I kende yow of kyssyng," quoþ þe clere þenne,
1490 "Quere-so countenaunce is couþe quikly to clayme;
Þat bicumes vche a knyȝt þat cortaysy vses."
"Do way," quoþ þat derf mon, "my dere, þat speche,
For þat durst I not do, lest I deuayed were;
If I were werned, I were wrang, iwysse, ȝif I profered."
1495 "Ma fay," quoþ þe meré wyf, "ȝe may not be werned,
ȝe ar stif innoghe to constrayne wyth strenkþe, ȝif yow lykeȝ,
ȝif any were so vilanous þat yow devaye wolde."
"ȝe, be God," quoþ Gawayn, "good is your speche,
Bot þrete is vnþryuande in þede þer I lende,
1500 And vche gift þat is geuen not with goud wylle.
I am at your comaundement, to kysse quen yow lykeȝ,

110

Full early she him beset

1475   His mood for to subdue.

She comes to the curtain,   and at the knight peeks.

Sir Wawain her welcomed,   worthily speaking first,

And she replies to him again   full eagerly in her words,

Sits her softly by his side,   and sweetly she laughs,

1480   And with a lovely look   she laid on him these words:

"Sir, if ye be Wawain,   it seems a wonder to me,

A warrior that is so well disposed   always doing good,

And can not of company   the customs understand,

And if one teaches you,   ye cast them from your

                                     mind.

1485   Thou hast forgotten already   what yesterday I taught

By the truest teaching   of talk that I know."

"What is that?" quoth the warrior,   "Indeed I knew never;

If it be sooth that ye say,   the blame is mine own."

"Yet I taught you of kissing,"   quoth the glowing one then,

1490   "Where-ever favor is known   quickly to claim it;

That becomes each knight   that courtesy uses."

"Do away," quoth that doughty man,   "my dear, that speech,

For that dare I not do,   lest I denied were;

If I were refused, I would be wrong,   indeed, if I proffered."

1495   "By my faith," quoth the merry one,   "ye can not be denied,

Ye are stout enough to constrain   with strength, if you like,

If any were so churlish   that she would deny you."

"Yea, by God," quoth Gawain,   "good is your speech,

But threat does not thrive   in the country where I live,

1500   And each gift that is not given   with good will.

I am at your commandment,   to kiss when you like,

3e may lach quen yow lyst, and leue quen yow þynkkeȝ,
      in space."
   Þe lady louteȝ adoun,
1505   And comlyly kysses his face,
   Much speche þay þer expoun
   Of druryes greme and grace.

   "I woled wyt at yow, wyȝe," þat worþy þer sayde,
   "And yow wrathed not þerwyth, what were þe skylle
1510   Þat so ȝong and so ȝepe as ȝe at þis tyme,
   So cortayse, so knyȝtyly, as ȝe ar knowen oute
   (And of alle cheualry to chose, þe chef þyng alosed
   Is þe lel layk of luf, þe lettrure of armes;
   For to telle of þis teuelyng of þis trwe knyȝteȝ,
1515   Hit is þe tytelet token and tyxt of her werkkeȝ,
   How ledes for her lele luf hor lyueȝ han auntered,
   Endured for her drury dulful stoundeȝ,
   And after wenged with her walour and voyded her care,
   And broȝt blysse into boure with bountees hor awen)
1520   And ȝe ar knyȝt comlokest kyd of your elde;
   Your worde and your worchip walkeȝ ayquere,
   And I haf seten by yourself here sere twyes;
   ȝet herde I neuer of your hed helde no wordeȝ
   Þat euer longed to luf, lasse ne more;
1525   And ȝe, þat ar so cortays and coynt of your hetes,
   Oghe to a ȝonke þynk ȝern to schewe
   And teche sum tokeneȝ of trweluf craftes.
   Why! ar ȝe lewed, þat alle þe los weldeȝ?

Ye may take one when you will,   and leave when you please,
  This place."
  The lady leans down,
1505   And comely kisses his face,
  Much speech they there expound
  Of Love's grief and grace.

"I want to know from you, warrior,"   that worthy there said,
"If you would not be angry there-with,   what was the reason
1510   That so young and so youthful   as ye at this time,
  So courteous, so knightly,   as ye are known all around
  (And since of all chivalry to choose,   the chief thing praised
  Is the loyal game of love,   the literature of arms;
  To tell of the trials   of these true knights,
1515   Are written tales   and great tomes on their works,
  How lads for their loyal loves   their lives have endangered,
  Endured for their dear ones   doleful adventures,
  And after were avenged by their valor   and their care averted,
  And brought blissfully into bower   by their own brave deeds).
1520   And ye are knight most comely   known of your age;
  Your word and your worship   are widely known,
  And I have sat here by yourself   two separate times;
  Yet heard I never that your head   held any words
  That ever belonged to love,   less nor more;
1525   And ye, that are so courteous   and clever about promises,
  Ought to a young thing   yearn to show
  And teach some examples   of true love crafts.
  Why! are ye unlettered,   who all the lauds wields?

Oþer elles ʒe demen me to dille your dalyaunce to herken?
1530   for schame!
    I com hider sengel, and sitte
    To lerne at yow sum game;
    Dos, techeʒ me of your wytte,
    Whil my lorde is fro hame."

1535 "In goud fayþe," quoþ Gawayn, "God yow forʒelde!
Gret is þe gode gle, and gomen to me huge,
Þat so worþy as ʒe wolde wynne hidere,
And pyne yow with so pouer a mon, as play wyth your knyʒt
With anyskynneʒ countenaunce, hit keuereʒ me ese;
1540 Bot to take þe toruayle to myself to trwluf expoun,
And towche þe temeʒ of tyxt and taleʒ of armeʒ
To yow þat, I wot wel, weldeʒ more slyʒt
Of þat art, bi þe half, or a hundreth of seche
As I am, oþer euer schal, in erde þer I leue,
1545 Hit were a folé felefolde, my fre, by my trawþe.
I wolde yowre wylnyng worche at my myʒt,
As I am hyʒly bihalden, and euermore wylle
Be seruaunt to yourseluen, so saue me Dryʒtyn!"
Þus hym frayned þat fre, and fondet hym ofte,
1550 For to haf wonnen hym to woʒe, what-so scho þoʒt elleʒ;
Bot he defended hym so fayr þat no faut semed,
Ne non euel on nawþer halue, nawþer þay wysten
       bot blysse.
    Þay laʒed and layked longe;
1555   At þe last scho con hym kysse.
    Hir leue fayre con scho fonge
    And went hir waye, iwysse.

Or else deem ye me too dull   your dalliance to heed?
1530   But stay!
         I come hither single, and sit
         To learn from you some play;
         Do, teach me of your wit,
         While my lord is away."

1535   "In good faith," quoth Gawain,   "God you reward!
         Great is the good glee,   and gladness to me huge,
         That so worthy as ye   would wend hither,
         And take pains for so poor a man,   and amuse your knight
         With any sort of attentions   recovers my ease;
1540   But to take the travail to myself   to expound true love,
         And tell the themes of texts   and tales of arms
         To you that, I know well,   wield more skill
         In that art, by the half,   or a hundred of such
         As I am, or ever shall be,   in earth where I live,
1545   It were a folly manifold, my fair,   by my troth.
         I would work your will   according to my power,
         As I am highly obligated,   and evermore will
         Be servant to yourself,   so save me Dear Lord!"
         Thus she tested that fair one,   and tempted him often,
1550   For to have won him to woe,   what-ever she thought else;
         But he defended him so fair   that no fault was seen,
         Nor of evil on either side,   naught did they know
              But bliss.
         They laughed and played for long;
1555   At the last she did him kiss.
         Her leave she did not prolong
         But went her way, with this.

Then ruþes hym þe renk and ryses to þe masse,
And siþen hor diner watჳ dyჳt and derely serued.

Þe lede with þe ladyeჳ layked alle day,
Bot þe lorde ouer þe londeჳ launced ful ofte,
Sweჳ his vncely swyn, þat swyngeჳ bi þe bonkkeჳ
And bote þe best of his bracheჳ þe bakkeჳ in sunder
Þer he bode in his bay, tel bawemen hit breken,

And madee hym mawgref his hed for to mwe vtter,
So felle floneჳ þer flete when þe folk gedered.
Bot ჳet þe styffest to start bi stoundeჳ he made,
Til at þe last he watჳ so mat he myჳt no more renne,
Bot in þe hast þat he myჳt he to a hole wynneჳ

Of a rasse bi a rokk þer renneჳ þe boerne.
He gete þe bonk at his bak, bigyneჳ to scrape,
Þe froþe femed at his mouth vnfayre bi þe wykeჳ,
Whetteჳ his whyte tuscheჳ; with hym þen irked
Alle þe burneჳ so bolde þat hym by stoden

To nye hym onferum, bot neჳe hym non durst
            for woþe;
        He hade hurt so mony byforne
        Þat al þuჳt þenne ful loþe
        Be more wyth his tusches torne,

Þat breme watჳ and braynwod bothe,

Til þe knyჳt com hymself, kachande his blonk,
Syჳ hym byde at þe bay, his burneჳ bysyde;
He lyჳtes luflych adoun, leueჳ his corsour,
Braydeჳ out a bryჳt bront and bigly forth strydeჳ,

Foundeჳ fast þurჳ þe forth þer þe felle bydeჳ.
Þe wylde watჳ war of þe wyჳe with weppen in honde,

Then the rider bestirs him   and rises to hear mass,
And dinner was ready   and decorously served.
1560   The lad with the ladies   delighted himself all day,
But the lord over the lands   galloped full oft,
Pursues this fierce swine,   that swings by the banks
And of the best of his hounds   bit the backs in two
Where he abode at bay,   until bow-men broke it out,
1565   And forced him, despite his heed,   to move farther out,
So many arrows there flew   when the folk gathered.
Yet at times he made the strongest   to start back,
Till at the last he was so tired   that he could no more run,
But in such haste as he could   he wends to a hole
1570   Of a ledge by a rock   where runs the stream.
He got the bank to his back,   begins to scrape the ground,
The froth foamed at his mouth,   foul by its corners,
Whets his white tusks;   with him then were angry
All the braves so bold   that by him stood
1575   To annoy him from afar,   but nigh him none dared
            Approach;
            He had hurt so many before
            That all were then full loath
            To be more with his tusks tore,
1580   By one fierce and brain-mad both,

Till the knight came himself,   spurring his bronc,
Saw him abide at bay,   his braves beside;
He lights lively adown,   leaves his courser,
Brandishes a bright broadsword   and boldly strides forth,
1585   Rushes fast through the stream   where the fierce one abides.
The beast was aware of the warrior   with weapon in hand,

117

Hef hyȝly þe here, so hetterly he fnast

Þat fele ferde for þe freke, lest felle hym þe worre.

Þe swyn setteȝ hym out on þe segge euen,

1590   Þat þe burne and þe bor were boþe vpon hepeȝ

In þe wyȝtest of þe water; þe worre hade þat oþer,

For þe mon merkkeȝ hym wel, as þay mette fyrst,

Set sadly þe scharp in þe slot euen,

Hit hym vp to þe hult, þat þe hert schyndered,

1595   And he ȝarrande hym ȝelde, and ȝedoun þe water

                ful tyt.

          A hundreth houndeȝ hym hent,

          Þat bremely con hym bite,

          Burneȝ him broȝt to bent,

1600   And doggeȝ to dethe endite.

There watȝ blawyng of "prys" in mony breme horne,

Heȝe halowing on hiȝe with haþeleȝ þat myȝt;

Brachetes bayed þat best, as bidden þe maystereȝ

Of þat chargeaunt chace þat were chef huntes.

1605   Þenne a wyȝe þat watȝ wys vpon wodcrafteȝ

To vnlace þis bor lufly bigynneȝ.

Fyrst he hewes of his hed and on hiȝe setteȝ,

And syþen rendeȝ him al roȝe bi þe rygge after,

Braydeȝ out þe boweles, brenneȝ hom on glede,

1610   With bred blent þerwith his braches rewardeȝ.

Syþen he britneȝ out þe brawen in bryȝt brode cheldeȝ,

And hatȝ out þe hastletteȝ, as hiȝtly bisemeȝ;

And tet hem halcheȝ al hole þe halueȝ togeder,

And syþen on a stif stange stoutly hem henges.

High bristled the hair,   so hatefully he snorted
That many feared for the fighter,   lest befell to him the worse.
The swine sets himself out,   straight at the stalwart,
1590   That the brave and the boar   were both in a heap
In the wildest of the water;   the worse had that other,
For the man marks him well,   as they met first,
Set firmly the sword   straight in the throat-slot,
Hit him up to the hilt,   that the heart sundered,
1595   And he, snarling, him yielded,   and went down in the water
          And sit.
               A hundred hounds at him went,
               That fiercely him bit,
               Braves to the open him sent,
1600   And dogs to death him commit.

There was blowing of "taken"   in many brave horns,
High hallooing on height   by horsemen that knew how;
Hounds bayed their best,   as bade their masters
Of that challenging chase   that were the chief hunters.
1605   Then a warrior   that was wise upon woodcraft
To carve this boar   lovingly begins.
First he hews off his head   and on high sets it,
And next rips him all rough   by the spine after,
Brings out the bowels,   burns them on coals,
1610   With bread blended there-with   to bestow on his hounds.
Next he butchers out the brawn   in bright broad slabs,
And has out the entrails,   as rightly befits;
And next fastens all whole   the halves together,
And then on a strong pole   stoutly them hangs.

1615   Now with þis ilk swyn þay swengen to home;
          Þe bores hed watȝ borne before þe burnes seluen
          Þat him forferde in þe forþe þurȝ forse of his honde
                 so stronge.
          Til he seȝ Sir Gawayne
1620   In halle hym þoȝt ful longe;
          He calde, and he com gayn
          His feeȝ þer for to fonge.

          Þe lorde ful lowde with lote and laȝter myry,
          When he seȝe Sir Gawayn, with solace he spekeȝ;
1625   Þe goude ladyeȝ were geten, and gedered þe meyny;
          He scheweȝ hem þe scheldeȝ, and schapes hem þe tale
          Of þe largesse and þe lenþe, þe liþerneȝ alse
          Of þe were of þe wylde swyn in wod þer he fled.
          Þat oþer knyȝt ful comly comended his dedeȝ,
1630   And praysed hit as gret prys þat he proued hade,
          For suche a brawne of a best, þe bolde burne sayde,
          Ne such sydes of a swyn segh he neuer are.
          Þenne hondeled þay þe hoge hed, þe hende mon hit praysed,
          And let lodly þerat þe lorde for to here.
1635   "Now, Gawayn," quoþ þe godmon, "þis gomen is your awen
          Bi fyn forwarde and faste, faythely ȝe knowe."
          "Hit is sothe," quoþ þe segge, "and as siker trwe
          Alle my get I schal yow gif agayn, bi my trawþe."
          He hent þe haþel aboute þe halse, and hendely hym kysses,
1640   And eftersones of þe same he serued hym þere.
          "Now ar we euen," quoþ þe haþel, "in þis euentide

1615   Now with this same swine   they swung toward home;
        The boar's head was borne   before the brave himself
        That defeated him in the ford   through force of his hand,
                So strong.
            Till he saw Sir Gawain
1620   In hall he thought it full long;
            He called, and Gawain came again
            For the share that to him belongs.

        The lord full loud with speech   and laughter merry,
        When he saw Sir Gawain,   with pleasure he speaks;
1625   The good ladies were gotten,   and the courtiers gathered;
        He shows them the shoulders,   and shapes for them the tale
        Of the largeness and the length,   and the loathsomeness also
        Of the war with the wild swine   in wood where he fled.
        That other knight full comely   commended his deeds,
1630   And praised it as great prowess   that he had proved,
        For such brawn of a beast,   the bold brave said,
        Nor such sides of a swine   saw he never ere.
        Then handled they the huge head;   the courtly one praised it,
        And let on he was jealous,   for the lord to hear.
1635   "Now, Gawain," quoth the good man,   "this game is your own
        By fine covenant and firm,   faithfully ye know."
        "It is sooth," quoth the stalwart,   "and as surely true
        All I got I shall give you in turn,   by my troth."
        He holds the horseman by the neck,   and honorably him kisses,
1640   And soon after of the same   he served him there.
        "Now are we even," quoth the horseman,   "in this eventide

Of alle þe couenauntes þat we knyt, syþen I com hider,
    bi lawe."

    Þe lorde sayde, "Bi Saynt Gile,

1645   Ʒe ar þe best þat I knowe!

    Ʒe ben ryche in a whyle,

    Such chaffer and Ʒe drowe."

Þenne þay teldet tableʒ trestes alofte,

Kesten cloþen vpon; clere lyʒt þenne

1650   Wakned bi woʒeʒ, waxen torches;

Seggeʒ sette and serued in sale al aboute;

Much glam and gle glent vp þerinne

Aboute þe fyre vpon flet, and on fele wyse

At þe soper and after, mony aþel songeʒ,

1655   As coundutes of Krystmasse and caroleʒ newe

With al þe manerly merþe þat mon may of telle,

And euer oure luflych knyʒt þe lady bisyde.

Such semblaunt to þat segge semly ho made

Wyth stille stollen countenaunce, þat stalworth to plese,

1660   Þat al forwondered watʒ þe wyʒe, and wroth with hymseluen,

Bot he nolde not for his nurture nurne hir aʒayneʒ,

Bot dalt with hir al in daynté, how-se-euer þe dede turned

    towrast.

    Quen þay hade played in halle

1665   As longe as hor wylle hom last,

    To chambre he con hym calle,

    And to þe chemné þay past.

Ande þer þay dronken, and dalten, and demed eft nwe

To norne on þe same note on Nwe Ʒereʒ euen

Of all the covenants we knitted   since I came hither,
        By law."
    The lord said, "By Saint Gile,
1645   Ye are the best that ever I saw!
    Ye will be rich in a while,
    If on such dealings ye draw."

Then they set up tables   on tops of trestles,
Cast cloths upon them;   clear light then
1650 Awakened on the walls,   in wax torches;
Stalwarts were seated and served   in the hall all about;
Sounds of gladness and glee   go up there-in
About the fire upon the floor,   and in many fine ways
At the supper and after,   many elegant songs,
1655 As songs of Christmas   and carols new
With all the mannerly mirth   that men may of tell,
And ever our lovely knight   the lady beside.
Such sweet looks to that stalwart   seemly she made
With still, stolen gestures,   that stalwart to please,
1660 That all in wonder was the warrior,   and wroth with himself,
But he would not, for his good manners,   merely deny her,
But dealt with her all in delicacy,   how-so-ever it seemed
        At last.
    When they were amused in hall
1665   As long as their will held fast,
    To chamber he did him call,
    And to the chimney they passed.

And there they drank, and dallied,   and decided again
To agree on the same conditions   for New Year's Eve

1670 Bot þe knyȝt craued leue to kayre on þe morn,
For hit watȝ neȝ at þe terme þat he to schulde.
Þe lorde hym letted of þat, to lenge hym resteyed,
And sayde, "As I am trwe segge, I siker my trawþe
Þou schal cheue to þe Grene Chapel þy charres to make,
1675 Leude, on Nw ȝereȝs lyȝt, longe bifore pryme.
Forþy þow lye in þy loft and lach þyn ese,
And I schal hunt in þis holt, and halde þe towcheȝ,
Chaunge wyth þe cheuisaunce, bi þat I charre hider;
For I haf fraysted þe twys, and faythful I fynde þe.
1680 Now 'þrid tyme þrowe best.' Þenk on þe morne,
Make we mery quyl we may and mynne vpon joye,
For þe lur may mon lach when-so mon lykeȝ."
Þis watȝ grayþely graunted, and Gawayn is lenged;
Bliþe broȝt watȝ hym drynk, and þay to bedde ȝeden
1685   with liȝt.
    Sir Gawayn lis and slepes
    Ful stille and softe al niȝt;
    Þe lorde þat his crafteȝ kepes,
    Ful erly he watȝ diȝt.

1690 After messe a morsel he and his men token;
Miry watȝ þe mornyng, his mounture he askes.
Alle þe haþeles þat on horse schulde helden hym after
Were boun busked on hor blonkkeȝ bifore þe halle ȝateȝ.
Ferly fayre watȝ þe folde, for þe forst clenged;
1695 In rede rudede vpon rak rises þe sunne,
And ful clere costeȝ þe clowdes of þe welkyn.
Hunteres vnhardeled bi a holt syde,
Rocheres roungen bi rys for rurde of her hornes;
Summe fel in þe fute þer þe fox bade,

1670	But the knight prayed leave to depart on the morn,
	For it was nearly the time that he should go.
	The lord prevented that, to stay longer him constrained,
	And said, "As I am stalwart knight, I stake my troth
	Thou shalt arrive at the Green Chapel thy affairs to settle,
1675	Liegeman, on New Year's first light, long before prime.
	Therefore lie thou in thy loft and take thine ease,
	And I shall hunt in this wood, and hold the terms,
	Exchange with thee the profit of what I acquire hither;
	For I have tested thee twice, and truthful I find thee.
1680	Now 'third time best throw.' Think on the morn,
	Make we merry while we may and be mindful of joy,
	For sorrow may one take whenever one likes."
	This was gracefully granted, and Gawain is delayed;
	Blithely brought was drink, and to bed they went
1685	With light.
	Sir Gawain lies and sleeps
	Full still and soft all night;
	The lord that his crafts keeps,
	Was ready at first daylight.
1690	After mass a morsel he and his men took;
	Merry was the morning; his mount he asks.
	All the horsemen that on horse hold the way him after
	Were ready, bestride their broncs, before the hall gates.
	Wonderfully fair was the field, for the frost clung;
1695	In red, ruddy upon clouds, rises the sun,
	And full clear coasted the clouds from the skies.
	Hunters unleashed hounds by a high wood's side,
	Rocks rang in the woods from the roar of their horns;
	Some found the scent in the track where the fox waited,

1700 Trayleȝ ofte a traueres bi traunt of her wyles;
A kenet kryes þerof, þe hunt on hym calles;
His felaȝes fallen hym to, þat fnasted ful þike,
Runnen forth in a rabel in his ryȝt fare,
And he fyskeȝ hem byfore; þay founden hym sone,
1705 And quen þay seȝe hym with syȝt þay sued hym fast,
Wreȝande hym ful weterly with a wroth noyse;
And he trantes and tornayeeȝ þurȝ mony tene greue,
Hauilouneȝ, and herkeneȝ bi heggeȝ ful ofte.
At þe last bi a littel dich he lepeȝ ouer a spenne,
1710 Steleȝ out ful stilly bi a strothe rande,
Went haf wylt of þe wode with wyleȝ fro þe houndes;
Þenne watȝ he went, er he wyst, to a wale tryster,
Þer þre þro at a þrich þrat hym at ones,
        al graye.
1715 He blenched aȝayn bilyue
And stifly start onstray,
With alle þe wo on lyue
To þe wod he went away.

Thenne watȝ hit list vpon lif to lyþen þe houndeȝ,
1720 When alle þe mute hade hym met, menged togeder:
Suche a sorȝe at þat syȝt þay sette on his hede
As alle þe clamberande clyffes hade clatered on hepes;
Here he watȝ halawed, when haþeleȝ hym metten,
Loude he watȝ ȝayned with ȝarande speche;
1725 Þer he watȝ þreted and ofte þef called,
And ay þe titleres at his tayl, þat tary he ne myȝt;
Ofte he watȝ runnen at, when he out rayked,
And ofte reled in aȝayn, so Reniarde watȝ wylé.

1700   And oft came upon it again   by the cunning of their wiles;
           A small hound cries there-of,   the huntsman on him calls;
           His fellows rush to him,   that panted full hard,
           Run forth in a rabble   on the right track,
           And the fox flees them before;   they found him soon,
1705   And when they saw him with sight   they pursued him fast,
           Denouncing him full wildly   with a wrathful noise;
           And he twists and turns   through many tough thickets,
           Doubles back, and hearkens   by hedges full oft.
           At the last by a little ditch   he leaps over a hedge,
1710   Steals out full silently   beside a small wood,
           Thought he escaped from the wood   by wiles for the hounds;
           Then he went, ere he was aware,   to a well-made blind,
           Where three fierce hounds thrust forth   and threaten him,
                    All gray.
1715   He bounded back from the strife
               And swiftly turned from the fray;
               With all the woe on life
               To the wood he went away.

           Then was it a pleasant life   to listen to the hounds,
1720   When all the pack had met him,   mingled together:
           Such a curse at that sight   they set on his head
           As if all the clustering cliffs had fallen,   clattered in heaps;
           Here he was hallooed,   when horsemen him met,
           Loud he was insulted   with snarling speech;
1725   There he was threatened   and often thief called,
           And always the hounds at his tail,   that he could not tarry;
           Often he was run at,   when he rushed out,
           And often ran back in again,   Reynard was so wily.

And ȝe! He lad hem bi lagmon, þe lorde and his meyny,
On þis maner bi þe mountes quyle myd-ouer-vnder,
Whyle þe hende knyȝt at home holsumly slepes
Withinne þe comly cortynes, on þe colde morne.
Bot þe lady for luf let not to slepe,
Ne þe purpose to payre þat pyȝt in hir hert,
Bot ros hir vp radly, rayked hir þeder
In a mery mantyle, mete to þe erþe,
Þat watȝ furred ful fyne with felleȝ wel pured,
No hweȝ goud on hir hede bot þe haȝer stones
Trased aboute hir tressour be twenty in clusteres;
Hir þryuen face and hir þrote þrowen al naked,
Hir brest bare bifore, and bihinde eke.
Ho comeȝ withinne þe chambre dore, and closes hit hir after,
Wayueȝ vp a wyndow, and on þe wyȝe calleȝ,
And radly þus rehayted hym with hir riche wordes,
with chere:
"A! mon, how may þou slepe?
Þis morning is so clere."
He watȝ in drowping depe,
Bot þenne he con hir here.

In dreȝ droupyng of dreme draueled þat noble,
As mon þat watȝ in mornyng of mony þro þoȝtes,
How þat destiné schulde þat day dele hym his wyrde
At þe Grene Chapel, when he þe gome metes,
And bihoues his buffet abide withoute debate more;
Bot quen þat comly com he keuered his wyttes,
Swenges out of þe sweuenes, and swareȝ with hast.

And yea! He led them by trickery,   the lord and his court,
1730 In this manner by the mountains   all mid-afternoon,
While the courtly knight at home   wholesomely sleeps
Within the comely curtains,   on the cold morn.
But the lady for love   did not let herself sleep,
Nor the purpose to pall   that was placed in her heart,
1735 But rose her up rapidly,   hurried herself thither
In a merry mantle,   reaching to the earth,
That was lined full fine   with fur well trimmed,
No good hues on her head   but the well wrought jewels,
Traced about her coif   in clusters of twenty;
1740 Her fair face and her throat   flaunted all naked,
Her breast bare before,   and behind also.
She comes within the chamber door,   and closes it her after,
Wide opens up a window,   and on the warrior calls,
And right away thus rebuked him   with her rich words,
1745   And cheer:
          "Ah! Man, how can thou sleep?
          This morning is so clear."
          He was in drowsing deep,
          But then he did her hear.

1750 In deep drowsing of dream   driveled that noble,
As man that was in mourning   for many sad thoughts,
How that destiny should that day   deal him his fate
At the Green Chapel,   when he the gallant meets,
And it behooves him his buffet   abide without debate;
1755 But when that comely came   he recovered his wits,
Swings out of the dreams,   and signs himself with haste.

Þe lady luflych com laȝande swete,
Felle ouer his fayre face, and fetly hym kyssed;
He welcumeȝ hir worþily with a wale chere.

1760 He seȝ hir so glorious and gayly atyred,
So fautles of hir fetures and of so fyne hewes,
Wiȝt wallande joye warmed his hert.
With smoþe smylyng and smolt þay smeten into merþe,
Þat al watȝ blis and bonchef þat breke hem bitwene,

1765 　　　and wynne.
　　　Þay lanced wordes gode;
　　　Much wele þen watȝ þerinne;
　　　Gret perile bitwene hem stod,
　　　Nif Maré hir knyȝt mynne.

1770 For þat prynces of pris depresed hym so þikke,
Nurned hym so neȝe þe þred, þat nede hym bihoued
Oþer lach þer hir luf, oþer lodly refuse.
He cared for his cortaysye, lest craþayn he were,
And more for his meschef ȝif he schulde make synne,

1775 And be traytor to þat tolke þat þat telde aȝt.
"God schylde," quoþ þe schalk, "þat schal not befalle!"
With luf-laȝyng a lyt he layd hym bysyde
Alle þe specheȝ of specialté þat sprange of her mouthe.
Quoþ þat burde to þe burne, "Blame ȝe disserue,

1780 Ȝif ȝe luf not þat lyf þat ȝe lye nexte,
Bifore alle þe wyȝeȝ in þe worlde wounded in hert,
Bot if ȝe haf a lemman, a leuer, þat yow lykeȝ better,
And folden fayth to þat fre, festned so harde
Þat yow lausen ne lyst and þat I leue nouþe;

The lady lovingly came,   laughing sweetly,
Bent over his fair face,   and fondly kissed him;
He welcomes her worthily   with warm good cheer.
1760   He saw her so glorious   and gayly attired,
So faultless of her features   and of such fine hues,
Strong welling joy   warmed his heart.
With smooth smiling and gentle   they settled into mirth,
That all was bliss and happiness   between them enjoyed,
1765   And then.
          They chattered words good;
          Much joy then was there-in;
          Great peril between them stood,
          But Mary kept her knight from sin.

1770   For that princess of excellence   pressed him so hard,
Pushed him so nigh the thread,   that by need he must
Either take there her love,   or loathly refuse.
He cared for his courtesy,   lest craven he were,
And more for his mischief   if he should make sin,
1775   And be traitor to that knight   that owned that castle.
"God be my shield," quoth the champion,   "that shall not be!"
With love-laughing a little   he laid aside
All speeches of affection   that sprang from her mouth.
Quoth that lady to the brave,   "Blame ye deserve,
1780   If ye love not that life   that ye lie next,
Before all the creatures   in the world wounded in heart,
Unless ye have a lady, a lover,   that you like better,
And have fixed your faith to that fine one,   fastened so hard
That you do not wish to loosen   and that I now believe;

1785 And þat ȝe telle me þat now trwly I pray yow,
For alle þe lufeȝ vpon lyue layne not þe soþe
for gile."
Þe knyȝt sayde, "Be Sayn Jon,"
And smeþely con he smyle;
1790 "In fayth I welde riȝt non,
Ne non wil welde þe quile."

"Þat is a worde," quoþ þat wyȝt, "þat worst is of alle;
Bot I am swared for soþe; þat sore me þinkkeȝ.
Kysse me now comly, and I schal cach heþen,
1795 I may bot mourne vpon molde, as may þat much louyes."
Sykande ho sweȝe doun and semly hym kyssed,
And siþen ho seueres hym fro, and says as ho stondes,
"Now, dere, at þis departyng do me þis ese:
Gif me sumquat of þy gifte, þi gloue if hit were,
1800 Þat I may mynne on þe, mon, my mournyng to lassen."
"Now iwysse," quoþ þat wyȝe, "I wolde I hade here
Þe leuest þing for þy luf þat I in londe welde,
For ȝe haf deserued, for soþe, sellyly ofte
More rewarde bi resoun þen I reche myȝt;
1805 Bot to dele yow for drurye þat dawed bot neked.
Hit is not your honour to haf at þis tyme
A gloue for a garysoun of Gawayneȝ gifteȝ,
And I am here an erande in erdeȝ vncouþe,
And haue no men wyth no maleȝ with menskful þingeȝ;
1810 Þat mislykeȝ me, ladé, for luf at þis tyme;
Iche tolke mon do as he is tan, tas to non ille
ne pine."
"Nay, hende of hyȝe honours,"
Quoþ þat lufsum vnder lyne,

1785   And that ye tell me now   truly I pray you,

For all the loves upon life   conceal not the truth

        For guile."

     The knight said, "By Saint John,"

     And smoothly did he smile;

1790   "In faith, I have right none,

     Nor none will have this while."

"That is a word," quoth that woman,   "that worst is of all;

But I am answered for sooth;   that seems painful for me.

Kiss me now, comely,   and I shall creep away,

1795   I may but mourn upon earth,   as maid that much loves."

Sighing she stooped down   and seemly him kissed,

And then she steps away from him,   and says as she stands,

"Now, dear, at this departing   do me this ease:

Give me something as thy gift,   thy glove as it were,

1800   That I may remember thee, man,   my mourning to lessen."

"Now indeed," quoth that warrior,   "I would I had here

The dearest thing for thy love   that I in this land possess,

For ye have deserved, for sooth,   awesomely often

More reward by reason   than I could reckon;

1805   But to give you for love   what would avail but little.

It is not to your honor   to have at this time

A glove for a keepsake   of Gawain's gifts,

And I am here on an errand   in earth unknown,

And have no men with no bags   of beautiful things;

1810   I mislike that, lady,   for love at this time;

Each trooper must do as he is told;   take it not as evil

        Nor decline."

     "Nay, courtier of high honors,"

     Quoth that lovely, fair and fine,

1815   "Þaȝ I hade noȝt of youreȝ,

           Ȝet schulde ȝe haue of myne."

      Ho raȝt hym a riche rynk of red golde werkeȝ,

      Wyth a starande ston stondande alofte

      Þat bere blusschande bemeȝ as þe bryȝt sunne;

1820   Wyt ȝe wel, hit watȝ worth wele ful hoge.

      Bot þe renk hit renayed, and redyly he sayde,

      "I wil no gifteȝ, for Gode, my gay, at þis tyme;

      I haf none yow to norne, ne noȝt wyl I take."

      Ho bede hit hym ful bysily, and he hir bode wernes,

1825   And swere swyfte by his sothe þat he hit sese nolde,

      And ho soré þat he forsoke, and sayde þerafter,

      "If ȝe renay my rynk, to ryche for hit semeȝ,

      Ȝe wolde not so hyȝly halden be to me,

      I schal gif yow my girdel, þat gaynes yow lasse."

1830   Ho laȝt a lace lyȝtly þat leke vmbe hir sydeȝ,

      Knit vpon hir kyrtel vnder þe clere mantyle,

      Gered hit watȝ with grene sylke and with golde schaped,

      Noȝt bot arounde brayden, beten with fyngreȝ;

      And þat ho bede to þe burne, and blyþely bisoȝt,

1835   Þaȝ hit vnworþi were, þat he hit take wolde.

      And he nay þat he nolde neghe in no wyse

      Nauþer golde ne garysoun, er God hym grace sende

      To acheue to þe chaunce þat he hade chosen þere.

      "And þerfore, I pray yow, displese yow noȝt,

1840   And letteȝ be your bisinesse, for I bayþe hit yow neuer

           to graunte;

        I am derely to yow biholde

        Bicause of your sembelaunt,

1815   "Though I have nothing of yours,
            Yet should ye have something of mine."

        She reached to him a rich ring   of red gold works,
        With a shining stone   standing aloft
        That bore blushing beams   like the bright sun;
1820   Know well it was worth   full huge wealth.
        But the rider refused it,   and readily he said,
        "I want no gifts, by God,   my gay, at this time;
        I have none you to offer,   and nothing will I take."
        She bade him full earnestly,   and he her offer rejects,
1825   And swore by his sooth   that he would not possess it,
        And she sorrowed that he forsook,   and said there-after,
        "If ye refuse my ring,   for it seems too rich,
        For ye would not so highly   be beholden to me,
        I shall give you my girdle;   that profits you less."
1830   She laid hold of a lace sash   wrapped lightly about her sides,
        Knotted upon her girdle   under the glowing mantle,
        Adorned it was with green silk   and with gold trimmed,
        Everything embroidered,   bedazzled by finger-work;
        And that she offered to the brave,   and blithely besought,
1835   Though it unworthy were,   that he would it take.
        And he said "nay"; he would not come nigh it   in any way,
        For neither gold nor treasure,   ere God him grace send
        To achieve the adventure   that he had chosen there.
        "And there-for, I pray you,   be not displeased,
1840   And lay aside your business,   for that bargain I will never
             It grant;
           I am deeply to you beholden
           For your kindness ever pleasant,

          And euer in hot and colde

1845   To be your trwe seruaunt."

"Now forsake ȝe þis silke," sayde þe burde þenne,
"For hit is symple in hitself? And so hit wel semeȝ.
Lo! So hit is littel, and lasse hit is worþy;
Bot who-so knew þe costes þat knit ar þerinne,
1850   He wolde hit prayse at more prys, parauenture:
For quat gome so is gorde with þis grene lace,
While he hit hade hemely halched aboute,
Þer is no haþel vnder heuen tohewe hym þat myȝt,
For he myȝt not be slayn for slyȝt vpon erþe."
1855   Þen kest þe knyȝt and hit come to his hert
Hit were a iuel for þe jopardé þat hym iugged were:
When he acheued to þe chapel his chek for to fech,
Myȝt he haf slypped to be vnslayn, þe sleȝt were
                        noble.
Þenne he þulged with hir þrepe and þoled hir to speke,
1860   And ho bere on hym þe belt and bede hit hym swyþe,
And he granted and hym gafe with a goud wylle
And bisoȝt hym, for hir sake, disceuer hit neuer,
Bot to lelly layne fro hir lorde; þe leude hym acordeȝ
Þat neuer wyȝe schulde hit wyt, iwysse, bot þay twayne
1865   for noȝte;
      He þonkked hir oft ful swyþe,
      Ful þro with hert and þoȝt.
      Bi þat on þrynne syþe
      Ho hatȝ kyst þe knyȝt so toȝt.

1870   Thenne lachcheȝ ho hir leue, and leueȝ hym þere,
For more myrþe of þat mon moȝt ho not gete.

And swear ever in hot or cold
1845   To be your true servant."

"Now forsake ye this silk," said the sweet lady then,
"For it is simple in itself? And so it well seems.
Lo! It is so little, and less is it worth;
But whosoever knew the qualities that are knitted there-in,
1850 He would it appraise at greater price, perchance:
Whatever gallant is girt with this green lace,
So long as he has it neatly fastened about,
There is no horseman under heaven to hew him that could,
For he can not be slain by any strategem upon earth."
1855 Then considered the knight, and it came to his heart
It would be a jewel for the jeopardy adjudged to him:
When he arrived at the chapel his fortune for to fetch,
Might he slip away and be unslain, the strategem would be
                noble.
Then he was patient with her speech and suffered her to speak,
1860 And she bore to him the belt and brought it to him swiftly
And he granted and she gave it with a good will
And besought him, for her sake, discover it never,
But loyally conceal it from her lord; the liegeman agrees
That never creature should it know, indeed, but those two
1865   For aught;
    He thanked her in speeches refined,
    Earnestly with heart and thought.
    By then, the third time,
    She has kissed the knight she caught.

1870 Then she takes her leave, and leaves him there,
For more mirth of that man could she not get.

When ho watʒ gon, Sir Gawayn gereʒ hym sone,
Rises and riches hym in araye noble,
Lays vp þe luf-lace þe lady hym raʒt,
1875   Hid hit ful holdely, þer he hit eft fonde.
Syþen cheuely to þe chapel choses he þe waye,
Preuély aproched to a prest, and prayed hym þere
Þat he wolde lyste his lyf and lern hym better
How his sawle schulde be saued when he schuld seye heþen.
1880   Þere he schrof hym schyrly and schewed his mysdedeʒ,
Of þe more and þe mynne, and merci besecheʒ,
And of absolucioun he on þe segge calles;
And he asoyled hym surely and sette hym so clene
As Domeʒday schulde haf ben diʒt on þe morn.
1885   And syþen he mace hym as mery among þe fre ladyes,
With comlych caroles and alle kynnes ioye,
As neuer he did bot þat daye, to þe derk nyʒt,
     with blys.
    Vche mon hade daynté þare
1890   Of hym, and sayde, "Iwysse,
    Þus myry he watʒ neuer are,
    Syn he com hider, er þis."

Now hym lenge in þat lee, þer luf hym bityde!
ʒet is þe lorde on þe launde ledande his gomnes.
1895   He hatʒ forfaren þis fox þat he folʒed longe;
As he sprent ouer a spenne to spye þe schrewe,
Þer as he herd þe howndes þat hasted hym swyþe,
Renaud com richchande þurʒ a roʒe greue,
And alle þe rabel in a res ryʒt at his heleʒ.
1900   Þe wyʒe watʒ war of þe wylde, and warly abides,
And braydeʒ out þe bryʒt bronde, and at þe best casteʒ.

138

When she was gone, Sir Gawain   readies himself soon,
Rises and arrays him   in noble raiment,
Stows away the love-sash   the lady him gave,
1875   Hid it full carefully,   where he could later find it.
Then quickly to the chapel   chooses he the way,
Privily approached a priest,   and prayed him there
That he would listen to his life   and learn him better
How his soul should be saved   when he set out hence.
1880   There he confessed him completely   and showed his misdeeds,
Of the mortal and the lesser,   and mercy beseeches,
And for absolution   he on the priest calls;
And he absolved him surely   and set him as clean
As if Doomsday had been destined   to dawn on the morn.
1885   And then he makes him as merry   among the fair ladies,
With comely carols   and all kinds of joy,
As never he did before that day,   to the dark night,
        With bliss.
    Each man had pleasure the more
1890   Of him, and said, "Sooth it is:
    Thus merry was he never before
    Since he came here, ere this."

Now let him linger in that place,   where love him betides!
Yet is the lord on the land   leading his gallants.
1895   He has killed this fox   that he followed long;
As he sprang over a hedge   to espy the scamp,
Where he heard the hounds   that hastened to him swiftly,
Reynard came rushing   through a rough grove,
And all the rabble in a rush   right at his heels.
1900   The warrior was aware of the wild,   and warily abides,
And brandishes the bright sword,   and at the beast strikes.

And he schunt for þe scharp, and schulde haf arered;
A rach rapes hym to, ryȝt er he myȝt,
And ryȝt bifore þe hors fete þay fel on hym alle,
1905 And woried me þis wyly wyth a wroth noyse.
Þe lorde lyȝteȝ bilyue, and lacheȝ hym sone,
Rased hym ful radly out of þe rach mouþes,
Haldeȝ heȝe ouer his hede, haloweȝ faste,
And þer bayen hym mony braþ houndeȝ.
1910 Huntes hyȝed hem þeder with horneȝ ful mony,
Ay rechatande aryȝt til þay þe renk seȝen.
Bi þat watȝ comen his compeyny noble,
Alle þat euer ber bugle blowed at ones,
And alle þise oþer halowed þat hade no hornes;
1915 Hit watȝ þe myriest mute þat euer men herde,
Þe rich rurd þat þer watȝ raysed for Renaude saule
                with lote.
        Hor houndeȝ þay þer rewarde;
        Her hedeȝ þay fawne and frote;
1920 And syþen þay tan Reynarde,
        And tyruen of his cote.

And þenne þay helden to home, for hit watȝ niȝ nyȝt,
Strakande ful stoutly in hor store horneȝ.
Þe lorde is lyȝt at þe laste at hys lef home,
1925 Fyndeȝ fire vpon flet, þe freke þer-byside,
Sir Gawayn þe gode, þat glad watȝ withalle,
Among þe ladies for luf he ladde much ioye;
He were a bleaunt of blwe þat bradde to þe erþe,
His surkot semed hym wel þat softe watȝ forred,

140

And he shuns the sharp,   and should have escaped;
A hound rushes him to,   right ere he might go,
And right before the horse's feet   they fell on him all,
1905   And bit into this wily   with a wrathful noise.
The lord alights quickly,   and lays hold of him soon,
Snatched him full rapidly   out of the hounds' mouths,
Holds him high over his head,   halloos fast,
And there bay at him   many brave hounds.
1910   Huntsman hurried them thither   with horns full many,
Aye blowing "Taken!" rightly   till they the rider see.
By that time was come   his company noble,
All that ever bore bugle   blew at once,
And all these other hallooed   that had no horns;
1915   It was the happiest pack of hounds   that ever men heard,
The rich roar that there was raised   for Reynard's soul
       From throats.
    Their hounds they there reward;
    Their heads they fondle and dote;
1920   And then they take Reynard,
    And tear off his coat.

And then they headed home,   for it was nigh night,
Sounding full stoutly   in their strong horns.
The lord is alighted at last   at his beloved home,
1925   Finds fire upon floor,   the fighter there-beside,
Sir Gawain the good,   that glad was withal,
Among the ladies for love   he led much joy;
He bore a mantle of blue   that brushed the earth,
His surcoat became him well   that softly was furred,

1930   And his hode of þat ilke henged on his schulder,

Blande al of blaunner were boþe al aboute.

He meteʒ me þis godmon inmyddeʒ þe flore,

And al with gomen he hym gret, and goudly he sayde,

"I schal fylle vpon fyrst oure forwardeʒ nouþe,

1935   Þat we spedly han spoken, þer spared watʒ no drynk."

Þen acoles he þe knyʒt and kysses hym þryes,

As sauerly and sadly as he hem sette couþe.

"Bi Kryst," quoþ þat oþer knyʒt, "ʒe cach much sele

In cheuisaunce of þis chaffer, ʒif ʒe hade goud chepeʒ."

1940   "ʒe, of þe chepe no charg," quoþ chefly þat oþer,

As is pertly payed þe chepeʒ þat I aʒte."

"Mary," quoþ þat oþer mon, "myn is bihynde,

For I haf hunted al þis day, and noʒt haf I geten

Bot þis foule fox felle — þe fende haf þe godeʒ! —

1945   And þat is ful pore for to pay for suche prys þinges

As ʒe haf þryʒt me here þro, suche þre cosses

        so gode."

       "Inoʒ," quoþ Sir Gawayn,

       "I þonk yow, bi þe rode,"

1950   And how þe fox watʒ slayn

       He tolde hym as þay stode.

With merþe and mynstralsye, with meteʒ at hor wylle,

Þay maden as mery as any men moʒten,

With laʒyne of ladies, with loteʒ of bordes.

1955   Gawayn and þe godemon so glad were þay boþe

Bot if þe douthe had doted, oþer dronken ben oþer.

Boþe þe mon and þe meyny maden mony iapeʒ,

1930   And his hood of that same   hanged on his shoulder,
            Bedecked all of ermine   were both all about.
            He meets this house-holder   in the middle of the floor,
            And all with gladness he him greeted,   and goodly he said,
            "Now I shall first   fulfill our agreement,
1935   That we speedily spoke,   where spared was no drink."
            Then embraces he the knight   and kisses him thrice,
            As sweetly and seriously   as he knew how to set them.
            "By Christ," quoth that other knight,   "ye catch much joy
            In your profits in this business,   if ye got a good price."
1940   "Yea, of the price no bother,"   quoth promptly that other,
            "Since the prices that I owed   are fully paid."
            "Mary," quoth that other man,   "my account is behind,
            For I have hunted all this day,   and naught have I got
            But this foul fox fur   —the fiend have the profits!—
1945   And that is full poor for to pay   for such prized things
            As ye have pressed on me here earnestly,   such three kisses
                 So good."
                "Enough," quoth Sir Gawain,
                "I thank you, by the rood,"
1950   And how the fox was slain
                He told him as they stood.

            With mirth and minstrelsy,   with meals when they wanted,
            They made as merry   as any men could
            With laughing of ladies,   with light wit and jests.
1955   Gawain and the good man   so glad were they both
            As if the court had gone crazy,   or was drunk.
            Both the man and the courtiers   made many jokes,

Til þe sesoun watʒ seʒen þat þay seuer moste;
Burneʒ to hor bedde behoued at þe laste.
1960   Þenne loʒly his leue at þe lorde fyrst
Fochcheʒ þis fre mon, and fayre he hym þonkkeʒ:
"Of such a selly soiorne as I haf hade here,
Your honour at þis hyʒe fest, þe Hyʒe Kyng yow ʒelde!
I ʒef yow me for on of youreʒ, if yowreself lykeʒ,
1965   For I mot nedes, as ʒe wot, meue to-morne,
And ʒe me take sum tolke to teche, as ʒe hyʒt,
Þe gate to þe Grene Chapel, as God wyl me suffer
To dele on Nw ʒereʒ day þe dome of my wyrdes."
"In god fayþe," quoþ þe godmon, "wyth a goud wylle
1970   Al þat euer I yow hyʒt halde schal I redé."
Þer asyngnes he a seruaunt to sett hym in þe waye,
And coundue hym by þe downeʒ, þat he no drechch had,
For to ferk þurʒ þe fryth and fare at þe gaynest
        bi greue.
1975   Þe lorde Gawayn con þonk,
        (Such worchip he wolde hym weue),
        Þen at þo ladyeʒ wlonk
        Þe knyʒt hatʒ tan his leue.

With care and wyth kyssyng he carppeʒ hem tille,
1980   And fele þryuande þonkkeʒ he þrat hom to haue,
And þay ʒelden hym aʒayn ʒeply þat ilk;
Þay bikende hym to Kryst with ful colde sykyngeʒ.
Syþen fro þe meyny he menskly departes;
Vche mon þat he mette, he made hem a þonke
1985   For his seruyse and his solace and his sere pyne,
Þat þay wyth busynes had ben aboute hym to serue;

144

Till the season was seen   that they must separate;
Braves to their beds   it behooved at the last.
1960   Then humbly his leave   from the lord first
Fetches this fine man,   and fair he him thanks:
"For such a splendid sojourn   as I have had here,
The honor at this high feast,   the High King you reward!
I give you me to be your servant,   if yourself it pleases,
1965   For I must by necessity, as ye know,   leave in the morn,
If ye me give some trooper to teach me,   as ye promised,
The way to the Green Chapel,   if God will allow me
To do on New Year's day   the decree of my fate."
"In good faith," quoth the good man,   "with a good will
1970   All that ever I promised you   I shall readily hold."
There he assigns him a servant   to set him in the way,
And conduct him by the downs,   that he no trouble have,
For to travel through the forest   and fare the most direct way
                To achieve.
1975   Gawain the lord did thank
           (Much worship there-in he did weave),
           Then from those ladies of rank
           The knight has taken his leave.

With sorrow and with kissing   he converses with them,
1980   And full many hearty thanks   he urged them to have,
And they yield him in turn   eagerly the same;
They commend him to Christ   with full cold sighs.
Then from the court   he courteously departs;
Each man that he met,   he gave him a thank
1985   For his service, his amusement,   and his special pains,
That they had been busy with   to serve about him;

And vche segge as soré to seuer with hym þere
As þay hade wonde worþyly with þat wlonk euer.
Þen with ledes and lyʒt he watʒ ladde to his chambre
1990 And blyþely broʒt to his bedde to be at his rest.
ʒif he ne slepe soundyly say ne dar I,
For he hade muche on þe morn to mynne, ʒif he wolde,
        in þoʒt.
    Let hym lyʒe þere stille,
1995   He hatʒ nere þat he soʒt;
    And ʒe wyl a whyle be stylle
    I schal telle yow how þay wroʒt.

146

And each stalwart as sorry   to separate from him there
As if they had dwelt worthily   with that noble forever.
Then by lads and light   he was led to his chamber
1990   And blithely brought to his bed   to be at his rest.
If he slept soundly   I dare not say,
For he had much on the morn to muse upon,   if he would,
        In thought.
    Let him lie there still,
1995   He has nearly what he sought;
    And if ye will a while be still
    I shall tell you how they wrought.

IV

Now neȝeȝ þe Nw ȝere, and þe nyȝt passeȝ,
Þe day dryueȝ to þe derk, as Dryȝtyn biddeȝ;
2000 Bot wylde wedereȝ of þe worlde wakned þeroute,
Clowdes kesten kenly þe colde to þe erþe,
Wyth nyȝe innoghe of þe norþe, þe naked to tene;
Þe snawe snitered ful snart, þat snayped þe wylde.
Þe werbelande wynde wapped fro þe hyȝe,
2005 And drof vche dale ful of dryftes ful grete.
Þe leude lystened ful wel þat leȝ in his bedde;
Þaȝ he lowkeȝ his liddeȝ, ful lyttel he slepes;
Bi vch kok þat crue he knwe wel þe steuen.
Deliuerly he dressed vp, er þe day sprenged,
2010 For þere watȝ lyȝt of a laumpe þat lemed in his chambre;
He called to his chamberlayn, þat cofly hym swared,
And bede hym bryng hym his bruny and his blonk sadel;
Þat oþer ferkeȝ hym vp and fecheȝ hym his wedeȝ,
And grayþeȝ me Sir Gawayn vpon a grett wyse.
2015 Fyrst he clad hym in his cloþeȝ þe colde for to were,
And syþen his oþer harnays, þat holdely watȝ keped,
Boþe his paunce and his plateȝ, piked ful clene,
Þe ryngeȝ rokked of þe roust of his riche bruny;
And al watȝ fresch as vpon fyrst, and he watȝ fayn þenne
2020   to þonk;
    He hade vpon vche pece,
    Wypped ful wel and wlonk;
    Þe gayest into Grece,
    Þe burne bede bryng his blonk.

2025 Whyle þe wlonkest wedes he warp on hymseluen:
His cote wyth þe conysaunce of þe clere werkeȝ
Ennurned vpon veluet, vertuus stoneȝ

150

Now nighs the New Year,   and the night passes,
The day drives out the dark,   as the Dear Lord commands;
2000   But wild weathers of the world   awakened outside,
Clouds cast keenly   the cold to the earth,
With well enough of the north wind,   naked flesh to torment;
The snow shivered full sharply   and snapped at wild beasts.
The warbling wind whipped   down from the heights
2005   And drove each dale   full of drifts full great.
The liegeman listened right well   who lay in his bed;
Though he locks his lids,   very little he sleeps;
By each cock that crowed   he knew well the hour.
Directly he was up and dressed,   ere the day sprang,
2010   For there was light of a lamp   that illumined his chamber;
He called to his servant,   who quickly him answered,
And bade him bring his armor   and saddle his bronc;
That other hurries fast   and fetches him his garments,
And gets Sir Gawain ready   in a goodly manner.
2015   First he clad him in his clothes   the cold to ward off,
And then his other harness,   that honorably was kept,
His paunch-armor and his plates,   polished full bright,
The rings rubbed clean of the rust   from his rich mail;
And all fresh as when first new,   and he now fit
2020   To proceed.
He put on every piece,
With care and speed,
The gayest from here to Greece;
The brave bade bring his steed.

2025   Meanwhile in the most worthy weeds   he wrapped himself:
His coat with the heraldic arms   in the clever works
Adorning the velvet,   very powerful jewels

Aboute beten and bounden, enbrauded seme3,
And fayre furred withinne wyth fayre pelures.

2030 3et laft he not þe lace, þe ladie3 gifte;
Þat forgat not Gawayn for gode of hymseluen.
Bi he hade belted þe bronde vpon his bal3e haunche3,
Þenn dressed he his drurye double hym aboute,
Swyþe sweþled vmbe his swange swetely þat kny3t

2035 Þe gordel of þe grene silke; þat gay wel bisemed
Vpon þat ryol red cloþe þat ryche wat3 to schewe.
Bot wered not þis ilk wy3e for wele þis gordel,
For pryde of þe pendaunte3, þa3 polyst þay were,
And þa3 þe glyterande golde glent vpon ende3,

2040 Bot for to sauen hymself, when suffer hym byhoued,
To byde bale withoute dabate of bronde hym to were
            oþer knyffe.
        Bi þat þe bolde mon boun
        Wynne3 þeroute bilyue,

2045   Alle þe meyny of renoun
        He þonkke3 ofte ful ryue.

Thenne wat3 Gryngolet grayþe, þat gret wat3 and huge,
And hade ben soiourned sauerly and in a siker wyse;
Hym lyst prik for poynt, þat proude hors þenne.

2050 Þe wy3e wynne3 hym to and wyte3 on his lyre,
And sayde soberly hymself and by his soth swere3:
"Here is a meyny in þis mote þat on menske þenkke3:
Þe mon hem maynteines, ioy mot þay haue;
Þe leue lady on lyue — luf hir bityde;

2055 3if þay for charyté cherysen a gest,
And halden honour in her honde, þe Haþel hem 3elde

About stitched and sewn,   embroidered seams,
And fair furred inside   with fine pelts.
2030   Yet left he not the lace,   the lady's gift;
That forgot not Gawain   for good of himself.
When he had belted the sword   on his brawny haunches,
Then he draped his love-token   double him about,
Swiftly swaddled round his waist   sweetly that knight
2035   The girdle of green silk;   well befitted that gay
Upon that royal red cloth   that rich was to see.
But this same warrior wore not   this girdle for its wealth,
For pride of the pendants,   though polished they were,
And though the glittering gold   gleamed on the ends,
2040   But for to save himself,   when to suffer it him behooved,
To battle without broadsword   himself to defend,
        Nor knife.
      By then the bold was bound
      Quickly unto strife,
2045   And to that whole court of renown
      Gives thanks to all on life.

Then was Gringolet ready,   that great was and huge,
And had been stabled to his liking   and well cared for;
He wanted the prick of the spur,   that proud horse then.
2050   The warrior wends him to   and examines his hide,
And said soberly to himself   and by his sooth swears:
"There are courtiers in this castle   that care for noble customs:
The man that maintains them,   joy may he have;
And his dear lady on life—   may love her betide;
2055   Since they for charity   cherish a guest,
And hold honor in their hand,   the High God reward them,

Þat haldeʒ þe heuen vpon hyʒe, and also yow alle!
And ʒif I myʒt lyf vpon londe lede any quyle,
I schuld rech yow sum rewarde redyly, if I myʒt."
2060   Þenn steppeʒ he into stirop and strydeʒ alofte;
His schalk schewed hym his schelde, on schulder he hit laʒt,
Gordeʒ to Gryngolet with his gilt heleʒ,
And he starteʒ on þe ston, stod he no lenger
          to praunce.
2065   His haþel on hors watʒ þenne,
            Þat bere his spere and launce.
            "Þis kastel to Kryst I kenne:
            He gef hit ay god chaunce."

The brygge watʒ brayde doun, and þe brode ʒateʒ
2070   Vnbarred and born open vpon boþe halue.
Þe burne blessed hym bilyue, and þe bredeʒ passed,
Prayses þe porter bifore þe prynce kneled —
Gef hym God and goud day, þat Gawayn he saue —
And went on his way with his wyʒe one,
2075   Þat schulde teche hym to tourne to þat tene place
Þer þe ruful race he schulde resayue.
Þay boʒen bi bonkkeʒ þer boʒeʒ ar bare,
Þay clomben bi clyffeʒ þer clengeʒ þe colde.
Þe heuen watʒ vphalt, bot vgly þer-vnder;
2080   Mist muged on þe mor, malt on þe mounteʒ;
Vch hille hade a hatte, a myst-hakel huge;
Brokeʒ byled and breke bi bonkkeʒ aboute,
Schyre schaterande on schoreʒ þer þay doun schowued.
Wela wylle watʒ þe way þer þay bi wod schulden,

He that holds the heaven on high,   and also you all!
And if I might life upon land   lead any longer,
I should render you some reward   readily, if I could."
2060   Then steps he into stirrup   and strides aloft;
His servant showed him his shield,   on shoulder he it laid,
Gives spur to Gringolet   with his gilt heels,
And he starts on the stone,   stood he no longer,
        To prance.
2065   The hero on horse was then,
        That bore his spear and lance.
        "This castle to Christ I commend.
        May He give it always good chance."

The bridge was brought down,   and the broad gates
2070   Unbarred and borne open   upon both sides.
The brave blessed himself quickly,   the planks crossed,
Praises the porter   that before the prince kneeled—
Gave him God and good day,   that Gawain he save—
And went on his way   with his one warrior,
2075   That should teach him to turn   to that terrible place
Where the rueful blow   he had to receive.
They bound by banks   where boughs are bare,
They climb by cliffs   where clings the cold.
The heaven was up high,   but ugly there-under;
2080   Mist drizzled on the moor,   melted on the mountains;
Each hill had a hat,   a huge mantle of mist;
Brooks boiled and broke   by banks about,
Brightly shattering on shores,   where they shot down.
Well wild was the way   where they went by wood.

2085   Til hit watȝ sone sesoun þat þe sunne ryses
            þat tyde.
      Þay were on a hille ful hyȝe
      Þe quyte snaw lay bisyde;
      Þe burne þat rod hym by
2090   Bede his mayster abide.

    "For I haf wonnen yow hider, wyȝe, at þis tyme,
    And now nar ȝe not fer fro þat note place
    Þat ȝe han spied and spuryed so specially after;
    Bot I schal say yow for soþe, syþen I yow knowe,
2095   And ȝe ar a lede vpon lyue þat I wel louy,
    Wolde ȝe worch bi my wytte, ȝe worþed þe better.
    Þe place þat ȝe prece to ful perelous is halden;
    Þer woneȝ a wyȝe in þat waste, þe worst vpon erþe,
    For he is stiffe and sturne, and to strike louies,
2100   And more he is þen any mon vpon myddelerde,
    And his body bigger þen þe best fowre
    Þat ar in Arþureȝ hous, Hestor, oþer oþer.
    He cheueȝ þat chaunce at þe Chapel Grene:
    Þer passes non bi þat place so proude in his armes
2105   Þat he ne dyngeȝ hym to deþe with dynt of his honde;
    For he is a mon methles, and mercy non vses,
    For be hit chorle oþer chaplayn þat bi þe chapel rydes,
    Monk oþer masseprest, oþer any mon elles,
    Hym þynk as queme hym to quelle as quyk go hymseluen.
2110   Forþy I say þe, as soþe as ȝe in sadel sitte,
    Com ȝe þere, ȝe be kylled, may þe knyȝt rede;

2085 It was soon the season   that the sun rises
               At that tide.
          They were on a hill full high,
          White snow lay them beside;
          The brave that rode him by
2090   Then bade his master abide.

     "For I have won your way hither,   warrior, at this time,
     And now are ye not far   from that noted place
     That ye have spied about and sought   with such special care;
     But I shall say you truly,   since well I know you,
2095 And ye are a lad upon life   that I well love,
     Would ye work by my wit,   ye would be the better.
     The place that ye press to   full perilous is held;
     A warrior dwells in that wasteland,   the worst on earth,
     For he is stout and stern,   and loves to strike,
2100 And mightier is he than any man   upon middle-earth,
     And his body bigger   than the best four
     That are in Arthur's house,   Hector or other.
     He keeps the custom   at the Green Chapel:
     There passes none by that place   so proud in his arms
2105 That he does not deal him death   by dint of his hand;
     For he is a man without measure,   and no mercy uses,
     For be it churl or chaplain   that by the chapel rides,
     Monk or mass-priest,   or any man else,
     He thinks it as good to kill him   as for himself to live.
2110 Therefore I say this,   as surely as ye in saddle sit,
     Come ye there, ye be killed,   if that knight has his way;

Trawe ȝe me þat trwely: þaȝ ȝe had twenty lyues
        to spende.
    He hatȝ wonyd here ful ȝore;
2115   On bent much baret bende,
    Aȝayn his dynteȝ sore
    ȝe may not yow defende.

"Forþy, goude Sir Gawayn, let þe gome one,
And gotȝ away sum oþer gate, vpon Goddeȝ halue!
2120 Cayreȝ bi sum oþer kyth, þer Kryst mot yow spede,
And I schal hyȝ me hom aȝayn, and hete yow fyrre
Þat I schal swere bi God and alle his gode halȝeȝ,
As help me God and þe halydam, and oþeȝ innoghe,
Þat I schal lelly yow layne, and lance neuer tale
2125 Þat euer ȝe fondet to fle for freke þat I wyst."
"Grant merci," quoþ Gawayn, and gruchyng he sayde:
"Wel worth þe, wyȝe, þat woldeȝ my gode,
And þat lelly me layne I leue wel þou woldeȝ.
Bot helde þou hit neuer so holde, and I here passed,
2130 Founded for ferde for to fle, in fourme þat þou telleȝ,
I were a knyȝt kowarde; I myȝt not be excused.
Bot I wyl to þe chapel, for chaunce þat may falle,
And talk wyth þat ilk tulk þe tale þat me lyste,
Worþe hit wele oþer wo, as þe wyrde lykeȝ
2135   hit hafe.
    Þaȝe he be a sturn knape
    To stiȝtel, and stad with staue,
    Ful wel con Dryȝtyn schape
    His seruaunteȝ for to saue."

Trust ye me truly;   though ye had twenty lives
     To spend.
    He has dwelt here since full yore;
2115   On earth many met their end
    Against him battling full sore;
    Ye cannot you defend.

"Therefore, good Sir Gawain,   let that gallant alone,
And go away some other way,   by God's wounds!
2120   Cross some other country,   where Christ may you help,
And I shall hasten me home again,   and assure you honestly
That I shall swear by God   and all his goodly saints,
As help me God, and the holy relics,   and many good oaths,
That I shall loyally lie for you,   and relate never a tale
2125   That ever ye fled for fear   from fighter that I knew."
"Great thanks," quoth Gawain,   and grudgingly he said:
"Well may thou prosper, warrior,   who wishes me good,
And loyally to lie for me   I believe well thou wouldest.
But held thou it never so hidden,   and I here slipped away,
2130   Fared for fear to flee,   in form that thou tell,
I would be a knight coward;   I could not be excused.
But I will go to the chapel,   whatever chance may befall,
And talk with that same knight   of whatever tale I want,
Be it weal or woe,   however fate will
2135   Behave.
    Though he be stern in fray,
    With a club to daunt the brave,
    The dear Lord can find a way
    His servants for to save."

2140   "Mary!" quoþ þat oþer mon, "now þou so much spelleȝ,
        Þat þou wylt þyn awen nye nyme to þyseluen,
        And þe lyst lese þy lyf, þe lette I ne kepe.
        Haf here þi helme on þy hede, þi spere in þi honde,
        And ryde me doun þis ilk rake bi ȝon rokke syde,
2145   Til þou be broȝt to þe boþem of þe brem valay;
        Þenne loke a littel on þe launde, on þi lyfte honde,
        And þou schal se in þat slade þe self chapel,
        And þe borelych burne on bent þat hit kepeȝ.
        Now fareȝ wel, on Godeȝ half, Gawayn þe noble!
2150   For alle þe golde vpon grounde I nolde go wyth þe,
        Ne bere þe felaȝschip þurȝ þis fryth on fote fyrre."
        Bi þat þe wyȝe in þe wod wendeȝ his brydel,
        Hit þe hors with þe heleȝ as harde as he myȝt,
        Lepeȝ hym ouer þe launde, and leueȝ þe knyȝt þere
2155   al one.
           "Bi Goddeȝ self," quoþ Gawayn,
           "I wyl nauþer grete ne grone:
           To Goddeȝ wylle I am ful bayn,
           And to hym I haf me tone."

2160   Thenne gyrdeȝ he to Gryngolet, and gedereȝ þe rake,
        Schowueȝ in bi a schore at a schaȝe syde,
        Rideȝ þurȝ þe roȝe bonk ryȝt to þe dale;
        And þenne he wayted hym aboute, and wylde hit hym þoȝt,
        And seȝe no syngne of resette bisydeȝ nowhere,
2165   Bot hyȝe bonkkeȝ and brent vpon boþe halue,
        And ruȝe knokled knarreȝ with knorned stoneȝ;
        Þe skweȝ of þe scowtes skayned hym þoȝt.
        Þenne he houed, and wythhylde his hors at þat tyde,
        And ofte chaunged his cher þe chapel to seche:

2140   "Mary!" quoth that other man,   "now thou so much speakest,
       That thou wilt thine own bane   bring on thyself,
       If thou want to lose thy life,   I look not to prevent thee.
       Have here thy helmet on thy head,   thy spear in thy hand,
       And ride thee down this same road   by yon rocky side,
2145   Till thou be brought to the bottom   of the broad valley;
       Then look a little at the open land,   on thy left hand,
       And thou shalt see in that glade   that same chapel,
       And the one brave in battle   that there thee bides.
       Now farewell, by God's wounds,   Gawain the noble!
2150   For all the gold upon ground   I would not go with thee,
       Nor bear thee fellowship through this forest   one foot further."
       With that the warrior in the wood   wrenches his bridle,
       Hit the horse with his heels   as hard as he could,
       Leaps him over the land,   and leaves the knight there
2155   Alone.
          "By God's self," quoth Gawain,
          "I will neither gripe nor groan;
          Of God's will I am certain,
          And I know that I am His own."

2160   Then gives he spur to Gringolet,   and gets again the path,
       Strikes in by a shore   at a shining wood's side,
       Rides through the rough bank   right to the dale;
       And then he watched about him   and wild he thought it,
       And saw no sign of refuge   nowhere beside,
2165   But high banks and steep   upon both sides,
       And rough knobs gnarled   with twisted stones;
       The clouds seemed to graze   on the clustered rocks.
       Then he halted, and held back   his horse at that tide,
       And often searched around   the chapel to seek:

2170 He seȝ non suche in no syde, and selly hym þoȝt,
Saue, a lyttel on a launde, a lawe as hit were;
A balȝ berȝ bi a bonke þe brymme bysyde,
Bi a forȝ of a flode þat ferked þare;
Þe borne blubred þerinne as hit boyled hade.

2175 Þe knyȝt kacheȝ his caple, and com to þe lawe,
Liȝeȝ doun luflyly, and at a lynde tacheȝ
Þe rayne and his riche with a roȝe braunche.
Þenne he boȝeȝ to þe berȝe, aboute hit he walkeȝ,
Debatande with hymself quat hit be myȝt.

2180 Hit hade a hole on þe ende and on ayþer syde,
And ouergrowen with gresse in glodes aywhere,
And al watȝ holȝ inwith, nobot an olde caue,
Or a creuisse of an olde cragge, he couþe hit noȝt deme
with spelle.

2185 We! Lorde," quoþ þe gentyle knyȝt,
"Wheþer þis be þe Grene Chapelle?
Here myȝt aboute mydnyȝt
Þe dele his matynnes telle!

"Now iwysse," quoþ Wowayn, "wysty is here;
2190 Þis oritore is vgly, with erbeȝ ouergrowen;
Wel bisemeȝ þe wyȝe wruxled in grene
Dele here his deuocioun on þe deueleȝ wyse.
Now I fele hit is þe fende, in my fyue wytteȝ,
Þat hatȝ stoken me þis steuen to strye me here.

2195 Þis is a chapel of meschaunce, þat chekke hit bytyde!
Hit is þe corsedest kyrk þat euer I com inne!"
With heȝe helme on his hede, his launce in his honde,
He romeȝ vp to þe roffe of þe roȝ woneȝ.

2170　He saw none such on any side,　and strange it seemed to him,
　　　　Except a little rise on a lawn,　a knoll as it were;
　　　　A smooth mound by a bank　beside the water's brim,
　　　　By a waterfall of a flood　that foamed up there;
　　　　The brook bubbled there-in　as if it were boilimg.
2175　The knight spurs his courser,　and comes to the mound,
　　　　Lights down lively,　and at a linden attaches
　　　　The reins of his steed　to a rough branch.
　　　　Then he bounds to the mound;　about it he walks,
　　　　Debating with himself　what it might be.
2180　It had a hole on the end　and on either side,
　　　　And overgrown with grass　on the ground everywhere,
　　　　And all was hollow within,　naught but an old cave,
　　　　Or a crevice of an old crag,　he could not say which
　　　　　　　　It befell.
2185　　　"Why! Lord," quoth the gentle knight,
　　　　　　"Can this be the Green Chapel?
　　　　　　Here might about midnight
　　　　　　The devil his matins tell!"

　　　　"Now indeed," quoth Wawain,　"it is wild here;
2190　This oratory is ugly,　with weeds overgrown;
　　　　Well befits the warrior　wrapped in green
　　　　To do here his devotion　in the devil's way.
　　　　Now I feel it is the fiend,　in my five wits,
　　　　That has doomed me on this date　to destroy me here.
2195　This is a chapel of misfortune;　may mischief betide it!
　　　　It is the cursedest church　that I ever came in!"
　　　　With high helmet on his head,　his lance in his hand,
　　　　He roams up to the roof　of the rough dwelling.

Þene herde he of þat hyȝe hil, in a harde roche

2200 Biȝonde þe broke, in a bonk, a wonder breme noyse,
Quat! hit clatered in þe clyff, as hit cleue schulde,
As one vpon a gryndelston hade grounden a syþe.
What! hit wharred and whette, as water at a mulne;
What! hit rusched and ronge, rawþe to here.

2205 Þenne "Bi Godde," quoþ Gawayn, "þat gere, as I trowe,
Is ryched at þe reuerence me, renk, to mete
      bi rote.
    Let God worche. We, loo!
    Hit helppeȝ me not a mote.

2210   My lif þaȝ I forgoo,
    Drede dotȝ me no lote."

Thenne þe knyȝt con calle ful hyȝe:
"Who stiȝtleȝ in þis sted me steuen to holde?
For now is gode Gawayn goande ryȝt here.

2215 If any wyȝe oȝt wyl, wynne hider fast,
Oþer now oþer neuer, his nedeȝ to spede."
"Abyde," quoþ on on þe bonke abouen ouer his hede,
"And þou schal haf al in hast þat I þe hyȝt ones."
ȝet he rusched on þat rurde rapely a þrowe

2220 And wyth quettyng awharf, er he wolde lyȝt;
And syþen he keuereȝ bi a cragge, and comeȝ of a hole,
Whyrlande out of a wro wyth a felle weppen,
A Deneȝ ax nwe dyȝt, þe dynt with to ȝelde,
With a borelych bytte bende by þe halme,

2225 Fyled in a fylor, fowre fote large.
Hit watȝ no lasse bi þat lace þat lemed ful bryȝt
And þe gome in þe grene gered as fyrst,
Boþe þe lyre and þe leggeȝ, lokkeȝ and berde,

164

Then heard he from that high hill,   on a hard rock
2200   Beyond the brook, in a bank,   a wondrous big noise,
Whoosh! It clattered in the cliff,   as if it cleave should,
As if one upon a grindstone   had ground a scythe.
Whoosh! It whirred and whirled,   as water at a mill;
Whoosh! It rushed and rang,   rueful to hear.
2205   Then "By God," quoth Gawain,   "that gear, as I believe,
Is readied to honor me,   to meet with due ritual the rider
            Coming here.
        Let God do as He will. Why, lo!
        No help for me will appear.
2210   My life though I forgo
        No noise will make me fear."

Then the knight   did call full loud:
"Who stands in this spot   my set date to keep?
For now is good Gawain   going right here.
2215   If any warrior wants anything,   let him wend hither fast,
Either now or never,   his errand to achieve."
"Abide," quoth one on the bank   above, over his head,
"And thou shalt have promptly   what I promised thee once."
Yet he raised that roaring noise   longer for a while
2220   And with whetting continued,   ere he would alight;
And then he climbed down by a crag,   and came from a hole,
Whirling out of a crevice   with a fierce weapon,
A Danish ax newly honed,   with which to yield the dint,
With a massive blade   curving back toward the handle,
2225   Filed sharp by a whetstone,   four foot long.
It was no less than that lace sash   that gleamed full bright,
And the gallant in the green   garbed as at first,
Both the face and the legs,   locks and beard,

Saue þat fayre on his fote he foundeȝ on þe erþe,

2230 Sette þe stele to þe stone, and stalked bysyde.

When he wan to þe watter, þer he wade nolde,

He hypped ouer on hys ax, and orpedly strydeȝ,

Bremly broþe on a bent þat brode watȝ aboute,

on snawe.

2235 Sir Gawayn þe knyȝt con mete;

He ne lutte hym noþyng lowe.

Þat oþer sayde, "Now, sir swete,

Of steuen mon may þe trowe."

"Gawayn," quoþ þat grene gome, "God þe mot loke!

2240 Iwysse þou art welcom, wyȝe, to my place,

And þou hatȝ tymed þi trauayl as truee mon schulde,

And þou knoweȝ þe couenaunteȝ kest vus bytwene:

At þis tyme twelmonyth þou toke þat þe falled,

And I schulde at þis Nwe ȝere ȝeply þe quyte.

2245 And we ar in þis valay verayly oure one;

Here ar no renkes vs to rydde, rele as vus likeȝ.

Haf þy helme of þy hede, and haf here þy pay.

Busk no more debate þen I þe bede þenne

When þou wypped of my hede at a wap one."

2250 "Nay, bi God," quoþ Gawayn, "þat me gost lante,

I schal gruch þe no grwe for grem þat falleȝ.

Bot styȝtel þe vpon on strok, and I schal stonde stylle

And warp þe no wernyng to worch as þe lykeȝ,

nowhare."

2255 He lened with þe nek, and lutte,

And schewed þat schyre al bare,

And lette as he noȝt dutte;

For drede he wolde not dare.

Save that fair on his foot   he fared on the earth,
2230   Set the steel to the stone,   and stalked beside.
When he got to the water,   where he would not wade,
He vaulted over on his ax   and vigorously strides,
Furiously fierce on a field   that flecked was about,
       With snow.
2235   Sir Gawain the knight did meet;
       He in no way bowed him low.
       That other said, "Now, sir sweet,
       That thou keepest thy word we know."

"Gawain," quoth that green gallant,   "May God guide thee!
2240   Indeed thou art welcome,   warrior, to my place,
And hast timed thy travail   as true man should,
And thou knowest the covenants   cast us between:
At this time twelvemonth   thou took what thee befell,
And I should at this New Year   surely thee requite.
2245   And we are in this valley   verily ourselves alone;
Here are no referees to interfere;   we may rule us as we like.
Have thy helmet off thy head,   and have here thy pay.
Make no more debate   than I brought thee then
When thou whipped off my head   with one single whack."
2250   "Nay," quoth Gawain,   "by God Who gave me soul,
I shall grudge thee not a bit   for any grief that may befall.
But be satisfied with one stroke,   and I shall stand still
And willingly I warrant   to work as thou please
       Anywhere."
2255   He leaned with the neck, to bow,
       And showed that flesh all bare,
       Let on that he naught feared now;
       For dread he would not despair.

Then þe gome in þe grene grayþed hym swyþe,
2260 Gedereȝ vp hys grymme tole Gawayn to smyte;
With alle þe bur in his body he ber hit on lofte,
Munt as maȝtyly as marre hym he wolde;
Hade hit dryuen adoun as dreȝ as he atled,
Þer hade ben ded of his dynt þat doȝty watȝ euer.
2265 Bot Gawayn on þat giserne glyfte hym bysyde,
As hit com glydande adoun on glode hym to schende,
And schranke a lytel with þe schulderes for þe scharp yrne.
Þat oþer schalk wyth a schunt þe schene wythhaldeȝ,
And þenne repreued he þe prynce with mony prowde wordeȝ:
2270 "Þou art not Gawayn," quoþ þe gome, "þat is so goud halden,
Þat neuer arȝed for no here by hylle ne be vale,
And now þou fles for ferde er þou fele harmeȝ!
Such cowardise of þat knyȝt cowþe I neuer here.
Nawþer fyked I ne flaȝe, freke, quen þou myntest,
2275 Ne kest no kauelacion in kyngeȝ hous Arthor.
My hede flaȝ to my fote, and ȝet flaȝ I neuer;
And þou, er any harme hent, arȝeȝ in hert;
Wherfore þe better burne me burde be called
                  þerfore."
2280   Quoþ Gawayn, "I schunt oneȝ,
          And so wyl I no more;
          Bot þaȝ my hede falle on þe stoneȝ,
          I con not hit restore.

"Bot busk, burne, bi þi fayth, and bryng me to þe poynt.
2285 Dele to me my destiné, and do hit out of honde,
For I schal stonde þe a strok, and start no more
Til þyn ax haue me hitte. Haf here my trawþe."
"Haf at þe þenne!" quoþ þat oþer, and heueȝ hit alofte,

168

Then the gallant in the green   got himself ready,
2260   Gathers up his grim tool   Gawain to smite;
With all the strength in his body   he bore it aloft,
Swung as mightily   as if to destroy him he would;
Had it driven down as deadly   as he pretended,
There had been dead of his dint   he that doughty was ever.
2265   But Gawain on that great ax   glanced sideways,
As it came crashing down   to the ground to destroy him,
And he shrank a little with the shoulders   from the sharp iron.
That other chevalier shifts   and the shining blade withholds,
And then reproved he the prince   with many proud words:
2270   "Thou art not Gawain," quoth the gallant,   "who is so good held,
That was never frightened by any host   by hill nor by vale,
And now thou flinchest for fear   ere thou feel harms!
Such cowardice of that knight   could I never hear.
I neither flinched nor fled,   fighter, when thou swung,
2275   Nor cast any quibbles   in the king's house of Arthur.
My head flew to my foot,   and yet fled I never;
And thou, ere any harm is had,   art horrified in heart;
Wherefore the better battler   I ought to be called
          Therefore."
2280   Quoth Gawain, "I flinched once alone,
          And so will I no more;
          But though my head fall on the stone,
          I cannot it restore.

"But get ready, battler, by thy faith,   and bring me to the point.
2285   Deal to me my destiny,   and do it out of hand,
For I shall stand thee one stroke,   and stir no more
Till thine ax have me hit.   Have here my troth!"
"Have at thee then!" quoth that other,   and heaves it aloft,

169

And waytez as wroþely as he wode were.

2290 He myntez at hym maȝtyly, bot not þe mon rynez,
Withhelde heterly his honde, er hit hurt myȝt.
Gawayn grayþely hit bydez, and glent with no membre,
Bot stode stylle as þe ston, oþer a stubbe auþer
Þat raþeled is in roché grounde with rotez a hundreth.

2295 Þen muryly efte con he mele, þe mon in þe grene:
"So, now þou hatȝ þi hert holle, hitte me bihous.
Halde þe now þe hyȝe hode þat Arþur þe raȝt,
And kepe þy kanel at þis kest, ȝif hit keuer may."
Gawayn ful gryndelly with greme þenne sayde:

2300 "Wy! þresch on, þou þro mon, þou þretez to longe;
I hope þat þi hert arȝe wyth þyn awen seluen."
"For soþe," quoþ þat oþer freke, "so felly þou spekez,
I wyl no lenger on lyte lette þin ernde
        riȝt nowe."

2305 Þenne tas he hym stryþe to stryke,
    And frounsez boþe lyppe and browe;
    No meruayle þaȝ hym myslyke
    Þat hoped of no rescowe.

He lyftes lyȝtly his lome, and let hit doun fayre
2310 With þe barbe of þe bitte bi þe bare nek;
Þaȝ he homered heterly, hurt hym no more
Bot snyrt hym on þat on syde, þat seuered þe hyde.
Þe scharp schrank to þe flesche þurȝ þe schyre grece,
Þat þe schene blod ouer his schulderes schot to þe erþe;
2315 And quen þe burne seȝ þe blode blenk on þe snawe,
He sprit forth spenne-fote more þen a spere
                        lenþe,

And looks about as wrathfully   as if he were crazy.

2290   He menaces at him mightily,   but not the man touches,
Withheld suddenly his hand,   ere it hurt might.
Gawain gracefully it abides,   and moved with no member,
But stayed still as the stone,   or a stump rather
That embedded is in rocky ground   with roots a hundred.

2295   Then merrily again did he speak,   the man in the green:
"So, now thou hast thy heart whole,   it behooves me to hit.
Help thee now the high rank   to which Arthur thee raised,
And preserve thy throat at this encounter,   if it protect can."
Gawain full grimly   with anger then said:

2300   "Why! thresh on, thou fierce man;   thou threatenest too long;
I believe that thy heart is frightened   by thine own self."
"For sooth," quoth that fighter,   "so fiercely thou speakest,
I will no longer look   to delay thine errand
       I vow."

2305   Then takes he his stance to strike,
      And frowns both lip and brow;
      No marvel that he it mislike,
      Who hoped for no help now.

He lifts lightly his tool,   and let it down fair

2310   With the blade of the bit   by the bare neck;
Though he hammered heartily,   he hurt him no more
Than a snick on that one side,   that slit the skin.
The sharp sank in the flesh   through the shining grease,
So that the bright blood over his shoulders   shot to the earth;

2315   And when the battler saw the blood   bright on the snow,
Feet together, he broad-jumped forth,   more than a spear's
                                                    length,

Hent heterly his helme, and on his hed cast,
Schot with his schuldereȝ his fayre schelde vnder,
Braydeȝ out a bryȝt sworde, and bremely he spekeȝ.
2320 Neuer syn þat he watȝ burne borne of his moder
Watȝ he neuer in þis worlde wyȝe half so blyþe.
"Blynne, burne, of þy bur, bede me no mo!
I haf a stroke in þis sted withoute stryf hent,
And if þow recheȝ me any mo, I redyly schal quyte,
2325 And ȝelde ȝederly aȝayn — and þerto ȝe tryst —
and foo.
Bot on stroke here me falleȝ;
Þe couenaunt schop ryȝt so,
Fermed in Arþureȝ halleȝ,
2330 And þerfore, hende, now hoo!"

The haþel heldet hym fro, and on his ax rested,
Sette þe schaft vpon schore, and to þe scharp lened,
And loked to þe leude þat on þe launde ȝede,
How þat doȝty, dredles, deruely þer stondeȝ
2335 Armed, ful aȝleȝ: in hert hit hym lykeȝ.
Þenn he meleȝ muryly wyth a much steuen,
And wyth a rynkande rurde he to þe renk sayde:
"Bolde burne, on þis bent be not so gryndel.
No mon here vnmanerly þe mysboden habbeȝ,
2340 Ne kyd bot as couenaunde at kyngeȝ kort schaped.
I hyȝt þe a strok and þou hit hatȝ, halde þe wel payed;
I relece þe of þe remnaunt of ryȝtes alle oþer.
Ȝif I deliuer had bene, a boffet paraunter
I couþe wroþeloker haf waret, to þe haf wroȝt anger.
2345 Fyrst I mansed þe muryly with a mynt one,
And roue þe wyth no rof-sore, with ryȝt I þe profered

172

Grabbed hastily his helmet,   and on his head cast,
Shot his shoulders   under his fair shield,
Brings out a bright sword,   and bravely he speaks.
2320   Never since that he was babe   born of his mother
Was there ever in this world   warrior half so blithe.
"Abide, battler;   of thy blows give me no more!
I have one stroke in this place   without strife taken,
And if thou offer me any more,   I readily shall requite,
2325   And repay rapidly in turn   —and there-to ye trust—
            As a foe.
        But one stroke here me befalls;
        The covenant shaped right so,
        Confirmed in Arthur's halls,
2330   And there-for, courtier, now whoa!"

The horseman held himself back,   and on his ax rested,
Set the shaft upon shore,   and on the sharp leaned,
And looked to the liegeman   that on the land went
How that doughty, dreadless,   dauntless there stands
2335   Armed, full fearless: in heart it pleases him.
Then he speaks merrily   with a mighty voice,
And with a ringing roar   he to the rider said:
"Bold battler, on this field   be not so fierce.
No man here unmannerly   thee mistreated has,
2340   Nor acted but as covenant   at king's court requires.
I promised a stroke and thou it hast;   hold thee well paid;
I release thee of the remnant   of all other rights.
If I more belligerent had been,   a buffet perhaps
I could more harshly have dealt,   to thee have wrought harm.
2345   First I menaced thee merrily   with one mighty blow,
And ripped thee with no gash;   which rightly I proffered

For the forewarde that we fest on the fyrst ny3t;
And þou trystyly þe trawþe and trwly me halde3;
Al þe gayne þow me gef, as god mon schulde.
2350 Þat oþer munt for þe morne, mon, I þe profered:
Þou kyssedes my clere wyf; þe cosse3 me ra3te3.
For boþe two here I þe bede bot two bare myntes
          boute scaþe.
     Trwe mon trwe restore,
2355   Þenne þar mon drede no waþe.
     At þe þrid þou fayled þore,
     And þerfor þat tappe ta þe.

"For hit is my wede þat þou were3, þat ilke wouen girdel,
Myn owen wyf hit þe weued, I wot wel for soþe.
2360 Now know I wel þy cosses, and þy costes als,
And þe wowyng of my wyf: I wro3t hit myseluen.
I sende hir to asay þe, and sothly me þynkke3
On þe fautlest freke þat euer on fote 3ede;
As perle bi þe quite pese is of prys more,
2365 So is Gawayn, in god fayth, bi oþer gay kny3te3.
Bot here yow lakked a lyttel, sir, and lewté yow wonted;
Bot þat wat3 for no wylyde werke, ne wowyng nauþer,
Bot for 3e lufed your lyf; þe lasse I yow blame."
Þat oþer stif mon in study stod a gret whyle,
2370 So agreued for greme he gryed withinne;
Alle þe blode of his brest blende in his face,
Þat al he schrank for schome þat þe schalk talked.
Þe forme worde vpon folde þat þe freke meled:
"Corsed worth cowarddyse and couetyse boþe!

For the agreement that we arranged   on the first night,
And thou, trusty and true,   thy troth to me heldest;
All the gains thou me gave,   as good man should.
2350   That second swing on this morning,   man, I proffered thee:
Thou kissedest my comely wife;   the kisses you returned to me.
For both of the two here I thee offered   only two bare swings
        To disconcert.
      A true man must truly restore;
2355   Then one need fear no hurt.
      At the third thou failed, no more;
      That tap is thy just desert.

"For it is my weed that thou wearest,   that same woven girdle,
Mine own wife weaved it for thee,   I know well for sooth.
2360   Now know I well thy kisses,   and thy customs also,
And the wooing of my wife: I wrought it myself.
I sent her to assay thee,   and soothly thou seemest to me
The most faultless fighter   that ever on foot went;
As pearl compared to the white peas   is greater in price,
2365   So is Gawain, in good faith,   compared to other gay knights.
But here you lacked a little, sir,   and loyalty you wanted;
But that was for no wild work,   nor wooing neither,
But for ye loved your life;   the less I you blame."
That other strong man in study   stood a great while,
2370   So aggrieved for anger   he groaned within;
All the blood of his breast   blended in his face,
That all he shrank for shame   as the chevalier talked.
The first word on the field   that the fighter spoke:
"Cursed be cowardice   and covetousness both!

2375 In yow is vylany and vyse þat vertue disstryeʒ."
Þenne he kaʒt to þe knot, and þe kest lawseʒ,
Brayde broþely þe belt to þe burne seluen:
"Lo! þer þe falssyng, foule mot hit falle!
For care of þy knokke cowardyse me taʒt
2380 To acorde me with couetyse, my kynde to forsake,
Þat is larges and lewté þat longeʒ to knyʒteʒ.
Now am I fawty and falce, and ferde haf ben euer
Of trecherye and vntrawþe: boþe bityde sorʒe
and care!
2385   I biknowe yow, knyʒt, here stylle,
         Al fawty is my fare;
         Leteʒ me ouertake your wylle
         And efte I schal be ware."

Thenn loʒe þat oþer leude and luflyly sayde:
2390 "I halde hit hardily hole, þe harme þat I hade.
Þou art confessed so clene, beknowen of þy mysses,
And hatʒ þe penaunce apert of þe poynt of myn egge,
I halde þe polysed of þat plyʒt, and pured as clene
As þou hadeʒ neuer forfeted syþen þou watʒ fyrst borne;
2395 And I gif þe, sir, þe gurdel þat is golde-hemmed,
For hit is grene as my goune. Sir Gawayn, ʒe maye
Þenk vpon þis ilke þrepe, þer þou forth þryngeʒ
Among prynces of prys, and þis a pure token
Of þe chaunce of þe Grene Chapel at cheualrous knyʒteʒ.
2400 And ʒe schal in þis Nwe ʒer aʒayn to my woneʒ,
And we schyn reuel þe remnaunt of þis ryche fest
ful bene."
Þer laþed hym fast þe lorde
And sayde: "With my wyf, I wene,

2375 In you is villainy and vice   that virtue destroys."
      Then he caught on to the knot,   and the clasp loosens,
      Flings, boiling, the belt   to the battler himself:
      "Lo! there the falsehood,   foul may it befall!
      For care of thy knock   cowardice me taught
2380 To accord me with coveting   my character to forsake,
      That is largesse and loyalty   that belongs to knights.
      Now am I faulty and false,   and feared have been ever
      Of treachery and untruth: both betide sorrow
              And care!
2385   I confess, knight; hear me still,
        I am at fault in this affair;
        Let me regain your good will
        And next time I shall be ware."

      Then laughed that other liege   and lovingly said:
2390 "I hold it happily healed,   the harm that I had.
      Thou hast confessed so cleanly,   told thy misdeeds,
      And hast the public penance   of the point of my blade ,
      I hold thee polished by that penance,   and purified as clean
      As if thou had never sinned   since thou was first born;
2395 And I give thee, sir,   the girdle that is gold-hemmed,
      For it is green as my gown.   Sir Gawain, ye may
      Think upon this thing,   when thou art in the throng
      Around princes of price,   and this a pure token
      Of the adventure of the Green Chapel   for chivalrous knights.
2400 And ye shall in this New Year   go again to my dwelling,
      And we shall revel for the remnant   of this rich feast
              The ladies between."
        Then invited him earnestly the lord
        And said: "With my wife, I ween,

2405   We schal yow wel acorde,

             Þat watʒ your enmy kene."

      "Nay, for soþe," quoþ þe segge, and sesed hys helme,

      And hatʒ hit of hendely, and þe haþel þonkkeʒ:

      "I haf soiorned sadly; sele yow bytyde,

2410   And He ʒelde hit yow ʒare þat ʒarkkeʒ al menskes!

      And comaundeʒ me to þat cortays, your comlych fere,

      Boþe þat on and þat oþer, myn honoured ladyeʒ,

      Þat þus hor knyʒt wyth hor kest han koyntly bigyled.

      Bot hit is no ferly þaʒ a fole madde,

2415   And þurʒ wyles of wymmen be wonen to sorʒe,

      For so watʒ Adam in erde with one bygyled,

      And Salamon with fele sere, and Samson eftsoneʒ:

      Dalyda dalt hym hys wyrde. And Dauyth þerafter

      Watʒ blended with Barsabe, þat much bale þoled.

2420   Now þese were wrathed wyth her wyles. Hit were a wynne

                             huge

      To luf hom wel, and leue hem not, a leude þat couþe.

      For þes wer forne þe freest, þat folʒed alle þe sele

      Exellently of alle þyse oþer, vnder heuenryche

           þat mused;

2425   And alle þay were biwyled

          With wymmen þat þay vsed.

          Þaʒ I be now bigyled,

          Me þink me burde be excused.

      "Bot your gordel," quoþ Gawayn, "God yow forʒelde!

2430   Þat wyl I welde wyth guod wylle, not for þe wynne golde,

      Ne þe saynt, ne þe sylk, ne þe syde pendaundes,

      For wele ne for worchyp, ne for þe wlonk werkkeʒ,

2405   We shall you well accord,

          That was your enemy keen."

      "Nay, for sooth," quoth the stalwart,   and seized his helmet,

      And has it off graciously,   and the Green Knight thanks:

      "I have sojourned sadly;   may good fortune be yours,

2410   And may He reward you   Who honors all good manners!

      And commend me to that courteous,   your comely companion,

      Both the one and that other,   mine honored ladies,

      Who their knight with their tricks   have cleverly beguiled.

      But it is no marvel   though a fool go mad,

2415   And through wiles of women   be won over to sorrow,

      For so was Adam on earth   by one beguiled,

      And Solomon by many such,   and Samson in his turn:

      Delilah dealt him his fate.   David there-after

      Was befuddled by Bathsheba   and much bale suffered.

2420   Now these were wronged by their wiles.   It would be a

                               gain

      To love them well, and believe them not,   if a lad could do so.

      For these were formerly the finest,   whom fortune favored

      Excellently over all these others,   under the heavens

          Confused;

2425   And all these made wild,

          By women that they used.

          Though I be now beguiled,

          I think I might be excused.

      "But your girdle," quoth Gawain,   "God give you reward!

2430   That will I wield with good will,   not for winning gold,

      Nor the sash, nor the silk,   nor the side pendants,

      For wealth nor for worship,   nor for the worthy works,

Bot in syngne of my surfet I schal se hit ofte,
When I ride in renoun, remorde to myseluen

2435 Þe faut and þe fayntyse of þe flesche crabbed,
How tender hit is to entyse teches of fylþe;
And þus, quen pryde schal me pryk for prowes of armes,
Þe loke to þis luf-lace schal leþe my hert.
Bot on I wolde yow pray, displeses yow neuer:

2440 Syn ʒe be lorde of þe ʒonder londe þer I haf lent inne
Wyth yow wyth worschyp; þe Wyʒe hit yow ʒelde
Þat vphaldeʒ þe heuen and on hyʒ sitteʒ.
How norne ʒe yowre ryʒt nome, and þenne no more?"
"Þat schal I telle þe trwly," quoþ þat oþer þenne,

2445 "Bertilak de Hautdesert I hat in þis londe.
Þurʒ myʒt of Morgne la Faye, þat in my hous lenges,
And koyntyse of clergye, bi craftes wel lerned,
Þe maystrés of Merlyn mony hatʒ taken
For ho hatʒ dalt drwry ful dere sumtyme

2450 With þat conable klerk, þat knowes alle your knyʒteʒ
        at hame;
    Morgne þe goddes
    Þerfore hit is hir name:
    Weldeʒ non so hyʒe hawtesse

2455 Þat ho ne con make ful tame.

"Ho wayned me vpon þis wyse to your wynne halle
For to assay þe surquidré, ʒif hit soth were
Þat rennes of þe grete renoun of þe Rounde Table;
Ho wayned me þis wonder your wytteʒ to reue,

2460 For to haf greued Gaynour and gart hir to dyʒe
With glopnyng of þat ilke gome þat gostlych speked
With his hede in his honde bifore þe hyʒe table.

But in sign of my sin   I shall see it often,
When I ride in renown,   remorse to myself,
2435   The fault and the feebleness   of the crabbed flesh,
How easy it is to entice   touches of filth;
And thus, when pride presses me on   for prowess of arms,
The look to this love-lace   shall allay my heart.
But one thing I would you pray,   may it displease you never:
2440   Since ye be lord of the yonder land   where I have lingered
With you with worship;   may the Warrior reward you
That upholds the heaven   and on high sits.
How say ye your true name?   And then I ask no more."
"That shall I tell thee truly,"   quoth that other then,
2445   "Bercilak de Hautdesert   I am called in this land.
Through might of Morgan la Fay,   who in my house lives,
And quaint lore of clergy,   by crafts well learned,
Many of the magic arts   of Merlin has she taken
For she was mistress   full dear at one time
2450   To that cunning clerk   that knows all your knights
            By fame;
        Morgan the goddess
        Therefore is her name:
        Wields none such high haughtiness
2455   Whom she cannot make full tame.

"She sent me in this manner   to your splendid hall
For to assay the swollen pride,   if it sooth were
That runs of the great renown   of the Round Table;
She brought thee this wonder   your wits to bereave
2460   And to have grieved Guenevere   and got her to die
By the gruesome sight of that gallant   that ghastly spoke
With his head in his hand   before the high table.

Þat is ho þat is at home, þe auncian lady;
Ho is euen þyn aunt, Arþureȝ half-suster,

2465 Þe duches doȝter of Tyntagelle, þat dere Vter after
Hade Arþur vpon, þat aþel is nowþe.
Þerfore I eþe þe, haþel, to com to þyn aunt,
Make myry in my hous; my meny þe louies,
And I wol þe as wel, wyȝe, bi my faythe,

2470 As any gome vnder God for þy grete trauþe."
And he nikked hym naye; he nolde bi no wayes.
Þay acolen and kyssen and kennen ayþer oþer
To þe prynce of paradise, and parten ryȝt þere
        on coolde;

2475   Gawayn on blonk ful bene
    To þe kyngeȝ burȝ buskeȝ bolde,
    And þe knyȝt in þe enker-grene
    Whiderwarde-so-euer he wolde.

Wylde wayeȝ in þe worlde Wowen now rydeȝ

2480 On Gryngolet, þat þe grace hade geten of his lyue;
Ofte he herbered in house and ofte al þeroute,
And mony aventure in vale, and venquyst ofte,
Þat I ne tyȝt at þis tyme in tale to remene.
Þe hurt watȝ hole þat he hade hent in his nek,

2485 And þe blykkande belt he bere þeraboute
Abelef as a bauderyk bounden bi his syde,
Loken vnder his lyfte arme, þe lace, with a knot,
In tokenyng he watȝ tane in tech of a faute.
And þus he commes to þe court, knyȝt al in sounde.

2490 Þer wakned wele in þat wone when wyst þe grete
Þat gode Gawayn watȝ commen, gayn hit hym þoȝt.

That is she that is at home,   the ancient lady;

She is even thine aunt,   Arthur's half-sister,

2465 The duchess' daughter of Tintagel,   whom dear Uther after

Had Arthur upon,   that glorious is now.

Therefore I urge thee, horseman,   to come to thine aunt,

Make merry in my house;   my court thee loves,

And I will love thee as well, warrior,   by my faith,

2470 As any gallant under God   for thy great truth."

And Gawain denied him with "nay";   he would in no way.

They embrace and kiss   and each the other

To the Prince of Paradise,   and they part right there

      In the cold;

2475   Gawain on bronco keen

    To the king's court rushes bold,

    And the knight in the deep green

    Went where-so-ever he would.

Wild ways in the world   Wawain now rides

2480 On Gringolet, when the grace   was given of his life;

Oft he was harbored in house   and often all outside,

And had many adventures on the way,   and vanquished oft,

Which I do not care at this time   in tale to rehearse.

The hurt was whole where he had been   hit in his neck,

2485 And the bright shining belt   he bore there-about

Obliquely as a baldric   bound by his side,

Locked under his left arm   the lace sash, with a knot,

As a token he was taken   by the touch of a sin.

And thus he comes to the court,   a knight all safe and sound.

2490 Joy wakened in that dwelling   when the great king was aware

That good Gawain was come   he thought it grand news.

Þe kyng kysseʒ þe knyʒt, and þe whene alce,
And syþen mony syker knyʒt þat soʒt hym to haylce,
Of his fare þat hym frayned; and ferlyly he telles,
2495 Biknoweʒ alle þe costes of care þat he hade,
Þe chaunce of þe chapel, þe chere of þe knyʒt,
Þe luf of þe ladi, þe lace at þe last.
Þe nirt in þe nek he naked hem schewed
Þat he laʒt for his vnleuté at þe leudes hondes
2500   for blame.
   He tened quen he schulde telle,
   He groned for gref and grame;
   Þe blod in his face con melle,
   When he hit schulde schewe, for schame.

2505 "Lo! lorde," quoþ þe leude, and þe lace hondeled,
"Þis is þe bende of þis blame I bere in my nek,
Þis is þe laþe and þe losse þat I laʒt haue
Of couardise and couetyse þat I haf caʒt þare;
Þis is þe token of vntrawþe þat I am tan inne,
2510 And I mot nedeʒ hit were wyle I may last,
For mon may hyden his harme, bot vnhap ne may hit,
For þer hit oneʒ is tachched twynne wil hit neuer."
Þe kyng comforteʒ þe knyʒt, and alle þe court als
Laʒen loude þerat, and luflyly acorden
2515 Þat lordes and ladis þat longed to þe Table,
Vche burne of þe broþerhede, a bauderyk schulde haue,
A bende abelef hym aboute of a bryʒt grene,
And þat, for sake of þat segge, in swete to were,
For þat watʒ acorded þe renoun of þe Rounde Table,

The king kisses the knight,   and the queen also,
And then many sure knights   that sought to embrace him,
That asked him how he fared;   and wonders he tells,
2495   He made known all the causes   of care that he had,
The achievement of the chapel,   the cheer of the knight,
The love of the lady,   the lace at the last.
The nick in the neck   he naked them showed
That he took from the liege lord's hands   for his disloyalty,
2500   To blame.
     He grieved when he had to tell;
     He groaned for grief and ill fame;
     In his face the blood did up well,
     When he showed the nick, for shame.

2505   "Lo! lord," quoth the liegeman,   and the lace handled,
"This is the emblem of the blame   I bear in my neck,
This is the injury and the loss   that I laid hold on
For cowardice and covetousness   that I have caught there;
This is the token of untruth   in which I was taken,
2510   And I must by necessity wear it   all the while I may live,
For one may hide his harm,   but sin can not be hidden,
For where it once is attached   depart will it never."
The king comforts the knight,   and all the court also
Laugh loudly there-at,   and lovingly agree
2515   That lords and ladies   that belonged to the Table,
Each member of the brotherhood,   a baldric should have,
 band obliquely him about   of a bright green,
And for the sake of that stalwart,   to wear that sign,
For it represents the renown   of the Round Table,

2520　And he honoured þat hit hade euermore after,
　　　　As hit is breued in þe best boke of romaunce.
　　　　Þus in Arthurus day þis aunter bitidde,
　　　　Þe Brutus bokeʒ þerof beres wyttenesse;
　　　　Syþen Brutus, þe bolde burne, boʒed hider fyrst,
2525　After þe segge and þe asaute watʒ sesed at Troye,
　　　　　　　iwysse.
　　　　　　Mony auntereʒ here-biforne
　　　　　　Haf fallen suche er þis.
　　　　　　Now þat bere þe croun of þorne,
2530　　　　He bryng vus to his blysse!

AMEN.
HONY SOYT QUI MAL PENCE.

2520	And he was honored that it had evermore after,
	As it is written in the best book of romance.
	Thus in Arthur's day this adventure befell,
	The Brutus books there-of bear witness;
	Since Brutus, the bold brave, first bounded hither
2525	Once the siege and the assault was ceased at Troy,
	As it is.
	Many adventures here-before
	Have fallen such as this.
	May He Who bore the crown of thorns
2530	Bring us to his bliss!"

AMEN.

SHAME TO HIM WHO THINKS EVIL.

Larry D. Benson is Higginson Professor of English Emeritus at Harvard University, where he taught for forty years, beginning in 1959, when he received his Ph.D. from the University of California at Berkeley and his appointment as an instructor at Harvard. He has written on a variety of subjects, including books on Middle English—*Art and Tradition in Sir Gawain and the Green Knight, King Arthur's Death,* and *Malory's Morte Darthure*—and articles on Old and Middle English, most notably his 1966 article "The Literary Character of Anglo-Saxon Formulaic Poetry." He is General Editor of *The Riverside Chaucer.*

Daniel Donoghue is the John P. Marquand Professor of English at Harvard University and the author of numerous publications on Old and Middle English, including *Lady Godiva: A Literary History of the Legend* and *Old English Literature: A Short Introduction.* He is editor of the Old English series for the Dumbarton Oaks Medieval Library of Harvard University Press.